STRIKES
Strikes
STRIKES

WALTER E. BAER

amacom A DIVISION OF AMERICAN MANAGEMENT ASSOCIATIONS

196588

Library of Congress Cataloging in Publication Data

Baer, Walter E
    Strikes : a study of conflict & how to resolve it.

    Includes bibliographical references and index.
    1. Arbitration, Industrial—United States.
2. Strikes and lockouts—United States. 3. Industrial relations—United States. I. Title.
HD5504.A3B3   331.89'2973   75-26713
ISBN 0-8144-5388-0

First Printing

To Suzy

PREFACE

THE PRESENT American scene is very different from the industrial world which most of us have known over the past quarter-century.

Until very recent years we were far and away the most sophisticated industrialized nation in the world. We were blessed with great natural resources, a tremendous, coherent domestic market, a technology superior to any in the world, a strong creditor position in world markets, the most respected currency in the world, and an enormous self-confidence about our capabilities.

Today's world looks very different, some of it, certainly, permanently so. The resurgent German and Japanese industrial economies can hold their own against us anywhere, and with England now in the Common Market, a unified Europe can be an enormous market and competitor. Our natural resources are dwindling, and for our oil, iron ore, and paper pulp we now depend heavily on imports. Our domestic market remains intact, except that foreign competition is much stiffer.

Our technology is superb, but the pressure for greater productivity continually erodes the employment base, and government, which furnished so much of the employment in the last ten years, is now cutting back or looking for technological aid in displacing costly employees. Our creditor position in world markets has changed to a serious debtor position for which we have not so far found a remedy. Our currency is under serious international pressure. And our self-confidence has been replaced by self-doubt.

It is against that unsettling backdrop that we must view the present state of our industrial relations. Few areas in the domestic life of the nation are vested with greater public concern. The need to develop better relations between organized labor and organized employers, and to integrate these relations with the interests of the nation as a whole, constitutes one of the most serious problems facing our economic and social system today.

It is true that, in large measure, labor and management have learned to respect *each other's* responsibilities: Management recognizes the union's function to advance the welfare of its constituency, and labor acknowledges the responsibility which a system of private ownership and free enterprise places on management—the responsibility to operate efficiently and profitably.

Labor and management compose an important and integral part of our industrial society. The growing complexities of that society and the instabilities of the international setting require that these parties to collective bargaining recognize not only each other's responsibilities and their own self-serving ones, but also their joint responsibility to society. This calls for improved private and public procedures and techniques and, above all, for an increased measure of maturity and wisdom.

The primary responsibility for such improvements lies with labor and management themselves. They must improve their methods for reconciling their separate and mutual interests with those of the larger community, and for reducing the extent of avoidable interruptions of operations.

By and large both parties have been adamantly opposed to contract arbitration in the past. Many individuals still are, but it is not so certain they should be, and the recent steel agreement represents a major breakthrough. Arbitration of labor disputes is not a panacea, but the other alternatives hold even less attraction at this point in time. Much as we might like to return to the past, we cannot do so. The collective bargaining process, including strikes and arbitration as we have known it, will not be immune to influence by the tides of change which now engulf us.[1]

We are presumably in an age of reason and enlightenment. It seems long past due for us to crawl out of our darkened industrial caves—leaving our clubs and other implements of war and force behind—into the light of a new day, where differences of men and institutions are resolved by the weight of reason, intelligence, common sense, and mutuality of purpose and goal.

Walter E. Baer

ix

CONTENTS

CONTENTS

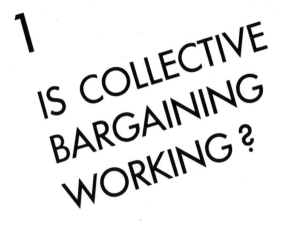

1

IS COLLECTIVE BARGAINING WORKING?

ONE OF THE cornerstones of the American economic system is the institution of collective bargaining. Collective bargaining as we know it can eventually include the use of the strike, labor's ultimate means of economic force. Of course, the strike is usually evoked as a last resort, presumably only when every other means of settlement has failed.

Recent statistics reveal an alarming trend: The number of strikes in the United States has been increasing steadily in recent years. For example, reports from the Department of Labor show that the number of walkouts rose almost 18 percent from 1969 to 1970, and the number of workers participating in those strikes increased by more than 77 percent.

Furthermore, strikes in the public sector are also on the upswing. In 1965 there were 42 strikes by public employees in this country as compared with 254—a sixfold increase—in 1968. Perhaps even more alarming are the statistics for the annual number of man-days lost in those years, 46,000 in 1965 as compared with 2,540,000 in 1968—a figure 55 times greater.[2]

The impact of such developments on the general public, as well as on employers, workers, and unions, cannot be denied. While there may be a philosophical dispute as to whether the system is working or not, for better or for worse, there can hardly be any argument as to the consequences whenever it fails to work.

The system failed to work, for example, in late 1969, when the General Electric Company and its electrical workers' union were unable to agree to a settlement when the old contract expired. That led to a companywide strike, directly affecting the well-being of more than 130 communities. About 130,000 company employees stopped work, crippling the operations of the nation's fourth largest industrial producer and second-ranked defense contractor.

Fortunately for everyone either involved or affected, neither party showed an interest in continuing the dispute with the unyielding ideological commitment of the participants in such infamous, to-the-bitter-end strikes as the Danbury Hatters (1902–1908) or Kohler (1954–1960), and the strike ended in February, 1970.

2

EFFECTS OF THE GE STRIKE

The General Electric settlement provided a reported wage increase of 74 cents to 79 cents per hour over 40 months on a wage base of $3.25. The annual percentage rise was 6.4 to 6.7. The average hourly increase in each 12-month period of the contract approximated 20 cents per hour. Consequently, the average employee, who had previously earned about $130 per week on a $3.25 per hour base, would now earn about $138 per week.

However, company officials estimated that the striking employees lost nearly $170 million in pay, or about $1,300 apiece. The average employee would have to work more than 4,000 hours (100 weeks) to make up this $1,300 loss before he could begin to enjoy the benefits of his negotiated increase.

Of course, the employees' wages were not the only losses caused by the strike. GE's earnings plummeted by 85 percent in the last quarter of 1969 as compared with the last quarter of the previous year, and the company was $42.6 million in the red for the first quarter of 1970.

As mentioned earlier, 130,000 workers were affected by the strike. If the average family unit includes five persons, then approximately three-fourths of a million persons were directly affected by this strike.

Of course, the $170 million lost in that year by the striking workers also meant a tax loss for the federal government. Assuming that each of the 130,000 workers filed a joint income tax return (a supposition which produces the most conservative

3

estimate possible), the government's tax loss was in the neighborhood of $24,050,000—a very nice neighborhood indeed. So much for the obvious, measurable consequences of the strike, which are relatively easy to identify as compared with less obvious ones.

For example, production delays caused by the strike may have inconvenienced many millions of people that year. Air conditioners were in shorter supply than usual, and some consumers may have been obliged to endure a hot summer without the refuge of an air conditioner. More serious repercussions may have resulted from delays in the delivery to utility companies of new turbines and other vital electrical equipment. Such delays could contribute to power shortages during periods of great demand and thus result in brownouts in affected regions.

The strike definitely contributed to the continuative woes of Long Island Rail Road commuters, because the delivery of new Budd cars was slowed by the delay in production of required parts. Those are only a few items in a list that could go on almost indefinitely.

What Was the GE Strike All About?

As too often happens when parties are in conflict, there was even disagreement as to what the GE dispute was really all about. The putative economic influence of any large company draws attention to its activities. Former Secretary of Labor George Schultz professed publicly to believe that the administration's fight against inflation influenced the issues of the strike. The managers at General Electric, he said, resisted larger wage increases as tenaciously as they did because

. . . they are feeling the effects of the anti-inflationary policy in their product market. They can't just raise their prices so easily. That means that their profits will be squeezed by a large wage increase. There's nothing so likely to put backbone into company negotiations as a squeeze on their profits. That's what is really going on there.

Not everyone agreed with the Secretary that the dispute turned on economic issues or owed its significance to them. A. H. Raskin of *The New York Times* compared the dispute to those between labor and management in the 1930s, when unions fought Tom Girdler of Republic Steel and Harry Bennett of Ford over the open shop. "The chief goal of the 14-union coalition," Raskin said, "was to slay Boulwarism, the papa-knows-best bargaining philosophy on which GE relied to dominate contract negotiations for two decades."

The writers and editors of *Time* agreed with Raskin. "In the minds of the strikers," they declared, "the primary issue was not even economic. Their aim was to force GE to abandon its bargaining strategy of 'Boulwarism' . . . which calls for management to make and stick to an initial 'firm, fair' offer. . . ."

The parties themselves asserted that the dispute involved much more than wages and that it transcended economic issues. As the strike began, a company spokesman declared:

The union leaders are striking because we have not increased the offer and it settles down to the union's idea of "ideological warfare." This does not suggest that the strike is for the benefit of employees. On the contrary, it suggests that it is a strike by union officials for their own particular purposes.

Unionists, both high and low, maintained that their fight was against an anti-union ideology of the company. George Meany of the AFL-CIO said: "This is a struggle against a company . . . determined to destroy not only the unions but the whole process of collective bargaining. Therefore, this is a fight for survival by the American trade union movement."

An officer of one of the unions involved echoed Meany's sentiments, arguing that GE's demands were "union-busting moves by the one major employer in the U.S. that persists in strikebreaking as a matter of policy."

So, not only were the parties engaged in a dispute, they also were in conflict as to what their dispute was all about. And it goes without saying that the most difficult kind of dispute to resolve is one in which the parties themselves cannot agree as to what they are quarreling about.

But rather than dwell on one situation alone, let us turn to the bigger picture by determining the implications of statistics for the nation's manufacturing industry compiled by the Bureau of Labor Statistics.[3]

OVERALL STRIKE LOSSES

The average hourly earnings of production workers in 1971 was $3.57. A conservative estimate of their average daily earnings would therefore be about $28. In 1971, strikes in this country involved 3.3 million workers and a total loss of 47.6 million man-days (the equivalent of one full year of employment by 183,000 people). The income lost from strikes in that year therefore totaled about $1.3 billion. Employed for a full year, 183,000 workers with average hourly earnings of $3.57 would have contributed approximately $219 million more in income tax payments.

The year 1961 also provides some interesting figures. Strikes in that year involved 1.45 million workers, with average hourly earnings of $2.32 and estimated average daily earnings of better than $18. With 16.3 million man-days lost (the equivalent of one year of full-time employment by 62,000 people), the total income lost was in the neighborhood of $293.5 million. The federal government in turn lost about $47.5 million in income taxes.

Now let us shorten what would otherwise be a long story by combining the data for the years 1961 and 1971 with that of the intervening years, 1962 through 1970. There was a total of 40,055 work stoppages in those 11 years, and 18.6 million workers were involved. The time lost came to 306.7 million man-days, lost income to more than $6.7 billion, and lost income tax to a conservative estimate of $1.2 billion.

Unfortunately, the statistics for those 11 years belie the claim that strikes are becoming less and less prevalent. For example, of the 306.7 million man-days lost due to work stoppages in the 11 years, the most recent years—1970 and 1971 —produced more than one-third of the total, or 114 million man-days. Those two years also contributed almost 11,000 work stoppages, or more than one-fourth of the 11-year total.

The income lost in 1970 and 1971, $3 billion, was almost half of the 11-year total, as was the two years' $450 million loss of federal income tax.

THE STRIKE: A TENACIOUS PROBLEM

The historical role of the union has been one of protest—against low wages, long hours, oppressive working conditions. The traditional instrument of protest has been the strike. The right to strike is sometimes advanced as one of the fundamental rights of a free society. In principle, this right, as well as the right to lock out, is now secure in the United States because the law recognizes its essentiality to collective bargaining.

As unions became more established, often as the result of strike action, collective bargaining prevailed and the use of the strike became more selective. Its use was limited primarily to those times when bargaining failed or when agreement could not be reached on the terms of a new contract.

Several years ago, observers were speculating that the United States might be witnessing a long-run decline in the use of the strike.[4] They thought that unions were resorting less often to the strike to achieve their objectives and predicted that more

8

and more bargaining agreements would be reached without strike action. While collective bargaining has reached a certain maturity over the years, particularly in situations where the parties have become more familiar with each other's point of view, it has not followed that the incidence of strikes has declined. Quite the contrary.

Moreover, fully one-third of these strikes occur during the life of the bargaining agreement and do not involve the negotiation of any subsequent agreement.[5] The number of such strikes is surprising considering the current widespread use of voluntary arbitration as a grievance settlement device. Although any strike is a protest action, it becomes more dramatic and rationally irreconcilable when it takes place at a time when an agreement is in effect with appropriate procedures to deal with whatever conditions gave rise to the dispute.

The problem of strikes, and of lockouts too for that matter, is that they obstruct the free flow of commerce and hence restrict competition among workmen, employers, sellers, and buyers. When great strikes occur, the right of the parties to resort to the ultimate weapons of economic warfare conflicts with the claims of the public to continued production and distribution of those goods and services deemed essential to health and safety.

But what constitutes an essential good and who is to decide? When is the public interest clearly threatened and who is to decide when it must supersede the private interests of the parties? How, in such cases, are private conflicts then to be resolved?

Merely to pose the questions is to indicate the

difficulty of framing an acceptable policy. Just as the union interest in wages and working conditions tends to spill over into the product market, conflicting with business and consumer interests, strikes may also affect the public interest in direct and costly ways.

As far as the great strike is concerned, any approach must be flexible and pragmatic rather than rigid and dogmatic. Fortunately, such an approach is feasible because of the obvious decline of emergency strikes in recent years. However, if centralized bargaining were to spread widely in times to come, the emergency problem would surely return, posing some hard choices for public policy.

LIMITATIONS ON THE RIGHT TO STRIKE

It has not been intended to give the reader the impression that the right to strike in the United States is without limits. It has in fact been limited, as to procedure and purpose, by common law and by legislation, notably the Labor Management Relations Act (1947).

The LMRA, more widely known as the Taft-Hartley Act, ushered in a new period of distinction between lawful and unlawful strikes. It represents an effort to limit strikes to those between primary disputants and those involving ends not considered by the framers of the Act to be improper. Unlawful strikes include, for example, those whose aim is the establishment of a closed shop or the recognition of a union not meeting the statutory conditions.

A strike is also unlawful under the Act if it violates procedural requirements, such as contractual no-strike clauses, express or implied. There must also be conformance to statutory periods of notice.[6]

At the present time there is no legislation providing for the compulsory settlement of labor disputes in private industry in the United States despite the recent trend toward heightened industrial conflicts. The national-emergency strike provisions of the Taft-Hartley Act and the cooling-off provision of the Railway Labor Act, which govern railroads and airlines, temporarily postpone the deleterious effects of prolonged work stoppages but include no element of compulsory adherence to governmentally determined employment standards.

The closest approximation to compulsory arbitration came in the form of a Nixon administration proposal which would have allowed railroad labor and management to bargain to an impasse and then required them to accept the fairest last offer as determined by a governmentally appointed arbitrator. However, Congress failed to implement this suggestion and to date, no new compulsory dispute settlement formulas have been advanced.

STRIKES IN THE PUBLIC SECTOR

Many strikes have a personal and disrupting impact on the public. For example, when a long strike caused the demise of the Newark (New Jersey) *News* in 1972, the public reacted angrily. Perhaps even more annoying of late have been the perennial teachers' strikes, labor crises involving firemen and policemen, and the stench-producing walkouts of sanitation workers. All of these bring a quick, adverse public reaction, yet they continue to occur.

Traditionally, in the minds of the public, a strike had meant action against a big bloodless, profitmaking corporation. However, when New York subway workers struck eight years ago and when Albert Shanker led New York City's teachers in a long, bitter, well-publicized strike several years ago, strikes came to be viewed as clearly against the public.[7]

There was a time, not so long ago, when work stoppages by government employees were beyond the pale. Calvin Coolidge considered them a form of anarchy and Franklin Roosevelt termed them "unthinkable." That attitude remained through the early sixties despite the establishment by then of a number of public-sector collective bargaining relationships and the actual occurrence of some work stoppages.

The federal government's policy toward work stoppages by its employees has been clearly spelled out in Section 19(b)(4) of Executive Order 11491, which makes it an unfair labor practice for a public employee labor organization to call or engage in a strike, work stoppage, or slowdown; to picket an agency in a labor-management dispute; or to condone any such activity by failing to take affirmative action to stop it. Just as explicit is 5 U.S.C. Section 7311(3) which provides in pertinent part that

An individual may not accept or hold a position in the Government of the United States or the government of the District of Columbia if he . . . (3) participates in a strike . . . against the Government of the United States or the government of the District of Columbia.

Several federal courts have enjoined federal employees from striking. In *Postal Clerks* v. *Blount,* a court rejected the union's argument that an absolute prohibition of strikes by federal employees was a denial of their First Amendment rights and equal protection of the law. With a few highly publicized exceptions in the last few years, the absolute ban on federal work stoppages has been respected by employee organizations.

The same condition certainly does not prevail in state and local governments today, despite the fact that all states clearly prohibit public-employee work stoppages by statute, court decision, or attorney general's opinion. In 1960 only 36 state and local public-sector strikes occurred throughout the United States as compared with a record high of 412 in 1970. The man-days lost in the two years were 58,400 and 2,023,300 respectively.[8] The fact that 19 of our 30 largest cities have contingency plans for work stoppages and that nine of the 19 have already used them provides another index of the extent of the problem.[9]

Over the last few years public-employee labor relations and collective bargaining have grown in importance in federal installations and in state and local government units. In late 1971 the Bureau of Labor Statistics reported that 1970 membership in unions and employee associations in the public sector had increased to a new high of 2.7 million and thus had continued the growth trend evident over the last few years. Most of the increase occurred among employees of state and local governments.[10]

Although with regard to frequency, number of workers involved, and man-days lost, strikes in public employment are insignificant in comparison with those in any other area of employment, they nevertheless pose a major problem in labor-management relations in the United States today. There are several reasons why relatively so few strikes should occasion so much concern:

1. Such strikes are specifically prohibited by the Taft-Hartley Act, by all states which have public-employment-relations laws, and by numerous court decisions. The willingness of so many otherwise law-abiding citizens to violate and defy the law poses a moral issue as well as a practical problem of dealing with such stoppages.

2. Many government services are vital to the normal functioning of the community. Strikes by policemen, firefighters, and prison guards are intolerable, and even the organizations to which these employees belong do not assert the right to strike. Strikes by hospital, sanitation, and public-utilities workers may present a threat to health or safety if they last more than a few days. Public transit, especially in a few large cities, is so important to the convenience and economic well-being of the people that many would classify it as an essential service. And strikes which close schools disrupt

the social, economic, and emotional lives of many people.

3. Strikes in public employment are bound to increase because government is the largest and fastest-growing industry in the United States and public employees are joining unions at a rapid rate. The total employment is soon expected to reach 15 million, with one out of every five employees working in government.

DISTORTION OF LABOR'S PUBLIC IMAGE

Perhaps more than anything else, organized labor's use of muscle in both the private and public sectors has hurt the public image of unions. Increasingly, labor's efforts are being interpreted as against the public interest, and even to those who consider themselves pro-union, labor's image is tending to become a bad caricature.

Polls conducted by Opinion Research Corporation (ORC), a McGraw-Hill subsidiary, point up the mood of the public:

Public opposition to the continued growth of unions, in membership and in power, has risen. Through the 1960s, 60 to 65 percent of those questioned said they felt that unions are too big or big enough. That figure rose sharply to 71 percent for the years 1970–1974.

More than half of the people polled in 1974 (55 percent, including 41 percent of the union members in the poll) said they felt unions have excessive power that should be curbed. On the other hand, another 14 percent believed that unions still are not strong enough to deal with today's powerful employers.

Most (68 percent, including 61 percent of the union members) felt strikes and labor disputes hurt the country. This attitude continued a trend upward that started in 1967.

A large percentage (59 percent, including 68 percent of the union members) blamed union demands and steadily rising labor costs for "causing the United States to price itself out of the world markets." And 68 percent (57 percent of the union members) blamed union wage settlements for causing higher prices.

The majority of the respondents (62 percent) believed unions should be more closely regulated, and 65 percent urged government intervention in big strikes.

The proportion who felt municipal employees should not be allowed to strike was down since 1968. Paradoxically, this was a period of rapid growth for public-employee and teacher unions. But the majority of those polled would have barred strikes by firemen (63 percent), policemen (62 percent), teachers (55 percent), and sanitation workers (54 percent). The percentages were just a little lower among union members.

As for whether labor leaders were meeting their responsibilities to the public, the consensus was that at best, they were doing only a fair job. They were rated "fair to poor" in those responsibilities by 64 percent of the general respondents. Among union members, they were rated "fair to poor" by 59 percent, "good" by 26 percent, and "excellent" by 8 percent, with the others declining to comment. The ORC's periodic surveys show that this dissatisfaction with labor leaders has been growing in recent years.[11]

ANSWERS TO SOME PERTINENT QUESTIONS

It will be worthwhile here to ask a few key questions whose answers should help to shed some light on needlessly obscure or troublesome areas of labor-management relations.

Does management overemphasize the importance of profits? That question is most suitably answered by another: Why is it that we seem to admire profit as a goal but deplore it as an achievement? From his experience and observations, the author is convinced that good profits not only accompany progress and make it manifest but also make important contributions to it. Profits must be regarded as essential to the promotion of economic growth and the achievement of desirable economic goals.

Do unions really raise wages? This may seem like a silly question because everyone knows of many cases where employers have complied with union demands for higher wages. But such instances do not really answer the question, and many economists would be inclined to reply in the negative. Maybe supply and demand would have produced the same raises in the market without the union.

Although any union man and most employers will tell you that of course unions raise wages, the

17

objective evidence is less clear. One careful study estimates that unions raised wages of their members by about 25 percent relative to nonunion workers in 1933 at the bottom of the depression (reflecting temporary union resistance to wage cuts), by about 5 percent in the inflationary boom of the late 1940s when all wages were bid up rapidly, and by 10 to 15 percent during the 1950s.[12]

Other studies generally confirm this modest, varying upward effect of unions on members' wages. The effect is greatest when market demand is weak. In prosperous periods of strong demand, market forces pull up nonunion wages about as fast as, or even faster than, those of union members.

The commonly cited but unconvincing claim is that union wages are by and large higher than nonunion ones. Many unionized industries, consisting of big companies with lots of skilled workmen, have had high wages even before they were unionized. It is true that there has been an increase in labor's share in the national income since the 1920s, when unions began to grow in size and number. However, that shift is not enough to provide clear evidence that unions have raised their members' aggregate share of wages.

Of course, even if a union did not succeed in giving its members an appreciably higher wage than nonunion workers receive, it would still be giving them other benefits.

What is the role of unions in our society? Our nation has had a long, successful experience in creating a democratic framework for our government and protecting the liberties of the individual.

The unions make a major contribution to our democratic industrial society by creating a two-party legislative system governing the life of the workplace. In their absence, the rules would be set exclusively by the employer.

Of course, our businesses are founded on the model of the individual entrepreneur making his own decisions, and no employer is expected to run his business on a democratic basis. However, there are certain democratizing influences, such as the fact that a business seldom has captive consumers. Nor does it have a captive labor force. Through their ability to choose employers, employees can have some influence on the nature of the rules under which they work. Through union membership, however, that influence can be increased considerably.

Also, unions usually insist on a grievance mechanism, and this brings a judicial process into industrial life which is more impartial than when the employer sits as both prosecutor and judge. Beyond that, unions create a new power center capable of standing against the power centers of the state and the corporation, both of which have grown much stronger in recent years. A rough balance among private and public power centers is the essence of a pluralistic society, and a pluralistic society is the only firm foundation for democracy in an economy based on industrial production.

How does the membership-ratification requirement create problems? Some years ago management negotiators generally could depend on a union's leaders to deliver a membership ratification if agreement was tentatively reached. The union negotiator might be an international representative, an international president, a local business agent, or some other spokesman. Management might get together with him in advance or at the appointed time, across the bargaining table or away from it. What really mattered was that if there was a meeting of minds, there was also some certainty that the agreement would hold up. Nowadays such a result is the exception rather than the rule.

The union practice of sending elected or selected representatives to the bargaining table possessed of certain positions and demands is in full accord with normal democratic procedures. However, the requirement that the membership ratify what its leaders have already agreed upon at the table goes far beyond such democratic practices.

If our congressmen or senators or governors do not do the job we the citizens elect them to do, we vote them out, but while they hold office, we abide by their decisions. Union members, however, do not permit their negotiators to come to the bargaining table fully empowered to consummate an agreement but rather authorize them only to make a tentative agreement. It has even happened that management has given the union's spokesmen everything its members had initially demanded, only to have the membership reject the offer anyway, much to the spokesmen's chagrin and embarrassment.

Spokesmen on both sides of the bargaining

table, the union ones included, feel that they must have the authority to make a final deal if the system is to work as it should. But, regrettably, the means of giving union representatives that authority are nowhere in sight at this time.

We have learned a great deal about industrial relations in the last three decades. Therefore, it seems unreal to observe the labor relations parties of today often behaving exactly as their predecessors did in the thirties. True, there is a *small* amount of evidence that they are still learning, and anything which can legitimately compress the learning and reaction times and improve the practice of collective bargaining is to be encouraged. All of the suggestions and ideas contained here are intended solely for that positive purpose.

THE $64 QUESTION

At this point it is superfluous to argue against either public-employee unionism or the right of government employees to use the strike. As has been noted, however, the use of such strikes has certainly not been eschewed despite the fact that they remain illegal in most jurisdictions. But there is one fairly reliable law about social processes: Things can never remain the same over long periods of time.

Collective bargaining today, like the social and economic climate in which it exists, is not the same as it was in post–World War II days. And in another 25 years it will not be what it is now. Should the employment of the strike continue in the years to come, particularly in the public sector, the public is going to become unanimous in the conviction that the strike is not the most rational way to settle labor disputes.

If we have learned anything from recent turbulent years, it is that the people vastly prefer order to chaos. They are growing tired of the now-familiar crisis of cities strangling in trash and garbage, or of public schools closing for intolerable periods, because a municipal government and a union cannot come to terms. Increasingly, they are going to ask why, when other kinds of disputes are settled in an orderly fashion, labor disputes cannot be.

Certainly there are important differences between strikes in government and those in private industry. At the same time, strikes by public and private employees have the same economic objectives—the improvement of wages, hours, and working conditions. Given the low salaries and poor conditions which often characterize employment in our schools, hospitals, social agencies, and other public services, one is loath to deprive these employees of any legitimate, reasonable means to improve their situation, unless it is clear that irreparable injury may result to the community at large.[13]

But the $64 question persists: Are the strike and the lockout the only means devisable by the public and private labor-management communities for effective, reasonable, and equitable disposition of their conflicts?

It is inconsistent that many who champion the punitive and violent strike technique for the settlement of both public and private labor disputes also advocate rational, responsible third-party techniques for the resolution of other kinds of social conflicts. Some of these conflicts are of a most deep-seated and emotional character, involving civil rights and ethnic differences. Rather than maintain these contradictory positions, it would make a great deal more sense to rely on rational processes in both areas of dispute.

In 1973 the national fund-raising drive to stamp out cancer produced $95 million. The income tax money lost by wages not paid during strikes in the years 1970 and 1971 was almost five times that amount.

In 1972 the national fund-raising drive to eliminate multiple sclerosis produced about $6 million. The income tax money lost due to strikes in the year 1971 was more than 36 times that amount. In fact, the tax loss from the previously mentioned General Electric strike alone accounted for more than four times the amount needed for multiple sclerosis research for one year.

In the handling of labor disputes we have now had the benefit of a long and varied kind of experience. Although we have developed promising alternatives to the strike, they are painfully slow in catching on. A few parties in private industry are choosing to use them, but regrettably such alternatives are vigorously opposed by many. Why do we slavishly pursue the course followed in the early days, even when it becomes exceedingly painful and undesirable, and especially when there are really effective alternatives?

2
THE PEACEMAKERS

PRESERVING collective bargaining—and the free and voluntary decision making which it represents—requires that representatives of labor and management fully realize their responsibilities. It has been said that "Industrial peace is not a God-given product. It must be cultivated and worked for constantly. . . ." [14] In other words, the privilege to agree or disagree on terms and conditions of employment can be preserved only if labor and management exercise it responsibly. And an important sign that they recognize their responsibilities is their willingness to rely on a third party to help settle their disputes.

In the United States that third party generally uses one of three tools which have been called "the marks of civilization. They are the enemies of distrust and force. They do away with the fang and claw." [15] Those tools are voluntary arbitration, mediation, and conciliation.

Federal policy has recognized the importance of the three methods as means of achieving industrial peace. Section 201 of the Labor Management Relations Act reads:

That it is the policy of the United States that—
(a) Sound and stable industrial peace and the advancement of the general welfare, health and safety of the nation and of the best interests of employer and employees can most satisfactorily be secured by the settlement of issues between employers and employees through the processes of conference and collective bargaining between employers and the representatives of their employees.

(b) The settlement of issues between employers and employees through collective bargaining may be advanced by making available full and adequate governmental facilities for conciliation, mediation *and voluntary arbitration* to aid and encourage employers and the representatives of their employees to reach and maintain agreements concerning rates of pay, hours, and working conditions, and to make all reasonable efforts to settle their differences by mutual agreement reached through conferences and collective bargaining or by such methods as may be provided for in any applicable agreement for the settlement of disputes. . . ."

This chapter will now examine those three labor-management tools, and later chapters will show how they (particularly arbitration) have been used to settle actual disputes.

VOLUNTARY ARBITRATION

The rapid growth of arbitration as a means of settling labor disputes has been one of the most important developments in industrial relations. In the United States today, about 94 percent of all collectively bargained agreements provide for binding arbitration as the ultimate step under labor-management grievance procedures. Arbitration provisions appear respectively in 95 and 97 percent of manufacturing and nonmanufacturing contracts. Only three industries fall below the 90 percent mark: construction (79 percent), primary metals (76 percent), and lumber (57 percent).[16]

In some countries, arbitration is imposed on labor and management by government edict. In the United States, however, it is a voluntary institution; that is, neither party is compelled to agree to include an arbitration provision in the labor contract. The fact that arbitration provisions are both voluntary and prevalent strongly indicates that the labor-management community considers arbitration, at best, successful and, at worst, acceptable.

Actually, from the point of view of both labor and management, the alternatives to arbitration are not very attractive. The parties to labor agreements could engage in industrial warfare to deal with their differences: They could strike, slow down, withhold production or jobs, or engage in sit-downs, work stoppages, lockouts, and myriad other self-destructive practices. Or they could turn to the courts of law, which are ill-equipped to cope with such matters and too far removed to have a sophisticated understanding of the problems peculiar to industrial disputants.

The labor arbitration process, on the other hand, does work. It may not be the most perfect creation of men, but to date no one has devised a more viable alternative.

Recent History of Arbitration

Arbitration has been called "the oldest known method of settlement of disputes between men." [17] It is known to have existed for many centuries prior to the establishment of English common law. More than 2,000 years ago, for example, King Solomon was acting as an arbitrator to settle disputes among his subjects. But we are concerned here with more recent history—the developments of the past 30 years—and their effect on the current state and style of arbitration practice.

In 1942, early in World War II, the National War Labor Board was created by presidential executive order and in 1943 it was provided statutory authority by the War Labor Disputes Act. During the war the Board resolved 20,000 disputes, the majority of them involving the provisions of collective bargaining agreements.

The policies of the Board contributed substantially to the advancement of labor arbitration in American industry, inasmuch as it required the parties to formulate contractual provisions for arbitrating their future disputes on applying and interpreting the labor agreement.[18] Today, as has been stated, the overwhelming majority of labor contracts provide for arbitration as the terminal point for disputes that remain unresolved after processing through the grievance machinery.

It was also during the Board's early days that a large number of our present arbitrators began their careers. Through the years these older arbitrators have accumulated a wealth of experience in the settlement of disputes, experience which has earned many of them respect and enviable reputations and has placed their services in great demand.

In 1947 the Federal Mediation and Conciliation Service (FMCS) was created by Section 202 of the Labor Management Relations Act, by which it was mandated to advance free collective bargaining as a means of attaining labor-management accord in the United States. The FMCS considers its arbitration services as an integral part of its efforts to fulfill that responsibility. (The FMCS is discussed in greater detail in other parts of this chapter.)

The Arbitrator's Function

Grievance arbitration derives its authority and effectiveness from the labor agreement. That document creates the grievance system, defines the authority of the arbitrator, and typically fixes substantive limits to the range of his decision making.

In relation to the agreement, there are three basic types of grievance matters that reach the arbitrator: (1) those involving conduct explicitly permitted or denied by the contract, (2) those evoked by vague or ambiguous language or by conflicting contract clauses, and (3) those with which the contract fails to deal.

With the first type, the clarity of the contract reduces the arbitrator's function to that of fact finder. The facts fall either within or outside the limits of the contract, and he has no choice but to comply with its language. With the second (probably the source of most grievance arbitrations), he can exercise considerable judgment. With the third, he must depend upon the source of his authority. If the parties limit his jurisdiction to the interpretation or application of the agreement, he obviously cannot rule on something beyond its scope. If they impose no such restriction, he is free to consider the equities.

Who Are the Arbitrators?

In spite of the rapidly increasing demand for their services, the average age of the really qualified arbiters in this country is about 60. The majority of these men received their initial arbitration experience serving on government labor boards during World War II and the Korean War.

As Robert Coulson aptly noted, parties engaging in the crystal-ball selection of arbiters "believe that their experience and judgment makes it possible for them to match the issue to the arbitrators much like the fisherman tempts the rainbow trout with the proper lure . . . one by-product of all this expertise is that practitioners become hesitant to accept an unknown quality." [19]

The extent of this hesitancy is reflected in recent statistics: (1) In 1971 over 75 percent of the cases processed under the auspices of the Federal Mediation and Conciliation Service were heard by arbiters representing only 25 percent of the FMCS roster. (2) Of the 1,475 arbiters on the national panel of the American Arbitration Association in

1970, only 458 actually rendered awards. And even among the 458 AAA arbiters, the distribution of cases per arbiter was uneven, as the following table shows:

Number of cases	1	2–5	6–10	11–20	21–30	31
Number of arbitrators rendering awards	142	149	69	50	24	24

The uneven distribution of cases is, of course, one of the factors which contribute to the high cost of arbitration and to the delay in having cases heard. Both costs and delays could be minimized by the greater use of apprentice arbitrators, who typically charge less in order to become established and are more readily available than their busier journeyman and professional associates. The vast majority of apprentices, though new to the role of rendering judgments as impartials, have had extensive experience in and exposure to the arbitration process.

A 1972 survey of 50 comparative newcomers who had been moderately active arbiters on the panels of the American Arbitration Association since 1960 reveals the following (the figures in parentheses correspond to the number of arbiters involved):

Range of ages: 34 to 65 years old

Range of experience on AAA panel of active service: 3 to 11 years

Previously employed by:

The National Labor Relations Board (10) *
Other federal agencies (17), including the War Labor Board and the Wage Stabilization Board (3)
City or state agencies (10)
Management or labor, or both (25)
American Arbitration Association (2)
Well-known impartial chairmen, as salaried assistants (7: these were among the most active of the 50 relatively new arbiters)
Education
Legal training (31) *
Degrees in the social sciences (27)
Degrees in industrial engineering (3)
Current occupation
Lawyer (15)
Educator (21)
Full-time arbitrator (12)
Industrial engineer (1)
Judge (1)
Previous occupations of the 12 (self-styled) full-time arbitrators
Assistant to an impartial chairman (4) *
Union official (1)
Employee of the New York State Mediation Board (3)
Employee of the NLRB (2: 1 who had recently retired and 1—the ex-union official—who had retired over 20 years ago)
Employee of the Massachusetts State Board, recently retired (1)

* Totals in parentheses exceed the total number of arbiters because of overlapping roles.

Corporation executive (1)
FMCS official and, for many years, labor
counsel for a large industry (1)
Lawyer (6)

Almost as one-sided as the case distribution among arbiters is their age distribution. The following table representing the age distribution of members of the National Academy of Arbitrators is revealing:

	1952	1962	1969
Under age 40	11.6%	4.7%	1.8%
Age 40 to 59	72.3	74.7	56.3
Age 60 and over	16.1	20.7	41.9

In 1952 the proportion of Academy arbiters at age 40 or older was 88.4 percent. In 1962 that figure had grown to 95.4 percent and in 1969 to an overwhelming 98.2 percent. On the other hand, by 1969 the under-40 group had all but disappeared. (The National Academy of Arbitrators as an institution will be discussed later in the chapter.)

Arbitrator Selection

In more than three-fourths of all agreements with arbitration clauses, selection of an arbiter is provided on an ad hoc, case-by-case basis. In 12 percent of all arbitration provisions a single arbitrator is designated to hear all cases which arise under the agreement's terms. The remaining contractual arrangements provide for establishment of a permanent board, designation of several umpires to serve on a rotational basis, or ad hoc selection from a list of arbitrators included in the contract.

Contracts of larger companies tend to provide for a permanent arbitrator (or board of arbitrators) whom the parties select and retain as long as he is mutually acceptable to them. Occasionally, the contract may also specify the selection of special arbiters, by agreement of the parties, for grievances that do not fall under the general arbitration procedure.

About 90 percent of all arbitration provisions require the parties to turn to an impartial agency should the selection process reach an impasse. That agency is most often the Federal Mediation and Conciliation Service or the American Arbitration Association. A small portion of agreements designate assistance from some other source, such as a state mediation agency or a federal or state judge.

With some overlapping, FMCS is appointed in approximately a third of the contracts, AAA in about 26 percent, and a small assortment of other agencies in 29 percent. Interestingly, 25 percent of labor agreements allow the impartial agency itself to appoint the arbitrator for their disputes, while about 50 percent state that the agency will be asked merely to provide a list of arbiter names from which the parties will make their own selection.

Both FMCS and AAA much prefer to provide a panel of names and let the parties take it from there; only when the parties are adamant—as in less than 3 percent of cases handled by FMCS

—will the agencies make the selection. The FMCS is discussed further in the following subsection.

The Federal Mediation and Conciliation Service

The FMCS is the principal federal agency with responsibilities in the field of labor arbitration. The regulations of the Service govern those cases between parties who have contractually agreed to utilize its arbitration services for the settlement of grievance disputes during the life of their agreement. The Service assists the parties by providing independent arbitrators qualified to hear cases at issue.

Once an arbitrator has been selected by the parties from nominees provided by the office of the FMCS General Counsel, the Service withdraws from active participation in the case, in recognition of the private nature of the relationship which exists between the parties and their arbitrator. However, the Service does retain an interest in the case to insure that it is being processed promptly and proceeds in accordance with FMCS regulations.

Growth in Demand for Arbitrators. Over the years requests from the private sector for qualified FMCS arbitrators have mounted dramatically. The following table indicates the arbitration unit workload of the FMCS in three representative fiscal years:

	1971	1967	1961
1. Requests for panels of nominees or direct appointments of arbitrators	12,327	6,955	3,174
2. Panels submitted	13,235	7,623	3,347

In the period from 1961 through 1971, both items 1 and 2 increased by almost 400 percent. The requests for panels reached a record annual level in 1971, and the figure of 12,327 represented a jump of 22.8 percent over the 1970 figure (not shown). The 13,235 panels provided by the Service in 1971 constituted an increase of 18.9 percent over the 1970 volume. And it must be remembered that each panel submitted consisted, on an average, of the names of seven arbiters. The size and scope of the FMCS program for providing arbiters thus begins to take some shape.

Reorganization of Services. Due to the growing demand for qualified arbiters and the problems attendant upon that growth, the FMCS arbitration services were reorganized in 1974. However, the specific objectives of the reorganization went beyond the need to provide more arbiters more efficiently. The objectives of the new program as a whole are listed as follows:

To improve arbitrator-selection and administrative procedures to expedite responses to requests from the parties and to achieve a maximum response time of one working day.

To create a flexible system which will absorb anticipated increases in arbitration requests while maintaining the new time standards. (Increases are anticipated from growth of activity in both private and public sectors of industrial relations.)

To distribute cases equitably among available arbitrators.

To develop the capacity to respond more effectively to requests for arbitrators with specific kinds of experience.

To identify national requirements for the development of new arbitrator resources.

To improve programs and policies by research to determine substantive trends in ad hoc arbitration.

The major thrust of the reorganization was provided by a new computerized data processing system, revision of administrative and monitoring procedures, and expansion of the scope of attention given arbitration matters by this agency.

The computerized information-retrieval system, called the FMCS Arbitrator Information Tracking System, or ARBIT, is a modification of a system developed in recent years by the National Aeronautics and Space Administration (NASA). The ARBIT system is capable of maintaining and producing data necessary for rapid, accurate arbitrator-panel selection. It has a virtually unlimited capacity for record storage and an ability to select arbitrator information from those records almost instantaneously.

Upon receipt of a request for a panel of arbitrators from disputing parties, the ARBIT system can supply the names of all the arbitrators on the roster who practice in or near the place where the arbitration is to be held and who meet other specific criteria, such as kinds of experience or skills.

A special feature incorporated into the system

is the automatic production of current biographical sketches, which accompany panel names sent to the parties. Such current information is important to those selecting arbitrators and to the arbitrators themselves; for the parties it insures more accurate evaluation and selection, and for the arbiters it insures an accurate, up-to-date presentation of their qualifications. This feature is especially important to newer arbiters, since their biographical sketches now immediately reflect each newly gained increment of experience.

The system is also able—through an automatic display of current case nominations, appointments, and awards with the name of each arbiter involved—to choose those arbiters who are, or will promptly be, available for hearings. This feature is designed to insure more equitable distribution of cases among available arbitrators and to avoid the continued use of those already burdened with case backlogs.

The ARBIT system also provides information on the special requirements of the parties and other data.

Types of Cases. The following is a list of the types and quantities of cases for which FMCS provided arbitration services in the fiscal year 1971:

	Number of Cases
General	
New or reopened contract terms	33
Contract interpretation or application	2,150
Issues	
Discharge and disciplinary actions	1,009
Incentive rates or standards	63

Issues	Number of Cases
Job evaluation	344
Promotion and upgrading	169
Layoff, bumping, and recall	208
Transfer	73
Other seniority issues	92
Overtime pay	151
Overtime distribution	178
Compulsory overtime	18
Union officers—superseniority and union business	23
Strike or lockout issues	18
Vacations and vacation pay	99
Holidays and holiday pay	85
Scheduling of work	147
Reporting, call-in and call-back pay	51
Health and welfare	34
Pensions	7
Other fringe benefits	65
Subcontracting	66
Jurisdictional disputes	31
Foreman, supervision, etc.	54
Mergers, consolidations, accretion, other plants	5
Working conditions, including safety	31
Miscellaneous	209

The National Academy of Arbitrators

Although the rosters of the AAA and FMCS arbitration panels abundantly number members of the National Academy of Arbitrators, the Academy is not an agency for the selection or appointment of arbitrators. It is rather a professional association whose purposes are, as the Academy's constitution (Article II, Section 1) states,

To establish and foster the highest standards of integrity, competence, honor, and character among those engaged in the arbitration of industrial disputes on a professional basis; to secure the acceptance of and adherence to the Code of Ethics for Arbitrators in Labor-Management Arbitration (being Part I of the Code of Ethics and Procedural Standards for Labor-Management Arbitration prepared by the American Arbitration Association and the National Academy of Arbitrators and approved by the Federal Mediation and Conciliation Service); to promote the study and understanding of the arbitration of industrial disputes; to encourage friendly association among the members of the profession; to cooperate with other organizations, institutions and learned societies interested in industrial relations, and to do any and all things which shall be appropriate in the furtherance of these purposes.

Membership. The National Academy of Arbitrators was founded in Chicago on September 14, 1947. As of 1972 the membership roster totaled approximately 375. Membership in the Academy is conferred by vote of the Board of Governors upon recommendation of the Membership Committee.

In considering applications for membership, the Academy applies the following standards: (1) The applicant should be of good moral character, as demonstrated by adherence to sound ethical standards in professional activities. (2) The applicant should have either substantial and current experience as an impartial arbitrator of labor-management disputes or (3) limited but current experience with general recognition—through scholarly publication or other activities—as an impartial authority on labor-management relations. In evaluating the applicant's experience, the Academy takes into account his general acceptability to the parties.

Membership is not conferred upon applicants who are primarily identified as advocates or consultants for labor or management in labor-management relations. The Academy, nevertheless, is aware of the fluid nature of the industrial relations field and the varied backgrounds and interests of its members. Therefore, it recognizes that the role of individual members and their availability as arbitrators may change from time to time. Some members may be called upon to serve as consultants to private or public organizations, some may act as advisors or advocates for labor or management, some may accept public office, and some may act in still other capacities that render them, for the time being, unavailable for service as arbitrators. The Academy does not consider that participation in such activities is necessarily inconsistent with continuous membership.

Because of the professional standards the Academy requires for membership and, therefore, the caliber of its members, both labor and management frequently seek out these individuals when making arbitral selections.

Activities. The Academy sponsors activities designed to improve the general understanding of the nature of arbitration and to promote its use as a means of settling labor disputes. It meets in national convention annually and, more often, in regional groupings. Such meetings are from time to time open to nonmembers.

The Academy maintains, in addition to its Membership Committee, the following standing committees: Executive; Ethics and Grievance; and Law and Legislation. A subject of continuing study and interpretation by the Ethics Committee is the Code of Ethics and Procedural Standards, jointly promulgated by the Academy and the American Arbitration Association.

For its members the Academy reprints lectures on various aspects of arbitration which have been delivered at its meetings. Each year it publishes an account of the proceedings of its annual meeting.[20]

MEDIATION AND CONCILIATION

Practically all writers in the labor relations field use the terms *mediation* and *conciliation* synonymously, to mean "the bringing together of employers and employees for a peaceable settlement of their differences by discussion and negotiation. The mediator, either a private or an official individual or board, makes inquiries without compulsory powers, trying to induce the two parties by mutual concessions to effect a settlement."

It should be recognized that that definition ignores a technical difference in meaning between the two words. *Conciliation* means simply to bring the two parties together to discuss their dispute. Strictly speaking, the third party, the conciliator, is confined to a passive role. *Mediation,* on the other hand, signifies an active role on the part of the third party, or mediator. He may act as a go-between and may even make suggestions for settling the dispute. This book will follow the prevalent usage, however, by ignoring that technical distinction and treating the terms as interchangeable.

Recent History of Mediation/Conciliation

The first mediation agencies in the United States were set up in the late 1880s by the states—not the federal government. In 1913 an act of Congress established an independent Department of Labor whose purpose was "to foster, promote, and develop the welfare of the wage earners of the United States, to improve their working conditions, and to advance their opportunities for profitable employment."

Among the duties the act bestowed on the Secretary of Labor was the "power to act as mediator and to appoint commissioners of conciliation in labor disputes whenever in his judgment the interests of industrial peace may require it to be done. . . ." The Department of Labor was thus charged with the difficult dual role of representing the interests of the wage earner and acting as an impartial mediator in labor disputes.

The first Secretary of Labor did not underestimate the importance of the peacemaker role. In his second annual report, he said: "Of all the functions of the Department of Labor which it is yet possible to administer, this one [mediation] may be reasonably regarded as the most important."

The United States Conciliation Service. With the coming of World War I, additional stress was thrown on labor relations, and the government reacted by multiplying its labor agencies. An outgrowth of this approach was the formation within the Labor Department of the Division of Conciliation and Labor Adjustment Service, later known as the United States Conciliation Service.

The industrial strife of the 1930s increased the burden of the Conciliation Service. The heightened industrial activity of World War II also brought labor difficulties, but many of these were handled by newly created agencies designed to cope with the unique problems of a wartime economy. Nevertheless, the dispute load of the Service increased tremendously.

The National Defense Mediation Board. By early in 1941 it was becoming apparent that the United States would be drawn into the war in Europe, and interruptions of defense production through labor disputes were becoming more and more intolerable to the government and the public. As a means of ending such disputes quickly, the President set up the National Defense Mediation Board by executive order on March 19, 1941.

The Board was made up of 11 members representing the public, the employers, and the employees. Its job was, basically, to try to settle those disputes affecting the defense effort which could not be settled by the commissioners of conciliation. When its mediation efforts failed and arbitration was refused, the Board was to make findings and recommendations for settlement. According to the executive order which created it, the Board's recommendations were not binding, but in actuality they were, since in three instances its decisions were enforced by the President through seizure of plants.

One of the basic weaknesses of the National

Defense Mediation Board was that it was placed simultaneously in the position of mediator and quasi arbitrator. Most, if not all, authorities on mediation feel that a mediation service loses its effectiveness when it also includes arbitration in its services.

Less than a year after the Board was established, its activities were brought to a virtual standstill by the resignation of its Congress of Industrial Organizations (CIO) members.

The Federal Mediation and Conciliation Service. Ever since the establishment of the Labor Department, its control over the federal mediation services had been seriously questioned. Opponents said that the Labor Department, dedicated by law to "the welfare of the wage earners of the United States," could not be a truly impartial mediator of disputes between labor and management. However, for more than 30 years they lacked the political leverage necessary to bring about the establishment of an independent mediation agency. That leverage was provided by the labor disputes of World War II.

With the strikes and strike threats that occurred during the war, the pendulum of public opinion began to swing away from organized labor, and the end of the war found the public in a definitely antilabor mood. Many people were convinced that the National Industrial Recovery Act (1931) and National Labor Relations Act (1935) had moved the government too far in the direction of labor and that something had to be done to redress the balance of power between labor and management.

Taking that argument as its mandate, Congress passed the Labor Management Relations Act (the Taft-Hartley Act) in 1947.

Among its many provisions, the LMRA set up a new mediation agency, the Federal Mediation and Conciliation Service. Unlike the United States Conciliation Service, which it replaced, the FMCS is completely independent of the Labor Department, thus eliminating the chief cause of criticism against its predecessor.

There are some other differences between the two agencies. The United States Conciliation Service had no jurisdictional limitations, whereas the FMCS is limited to disputes affecting interstate commerce. The new law also recognized the role of state and other mediation agencies, established limitations on the extent to which the FMCS could intercede in grievance disputes, and stated that the parties would be required to take part in meetings called by the Service.

Except for a time in World War II, the United States Conciliation Service had no efficient means of learning about disputes and, consequently, often did not know about a dispute until the positions of both sides had been cemented in misunderstanding. To avoid this, the new law made it mandatory for the party seeking to terminate or modify its contract to contact the other party 60 days before the proposed date of change and offer to meet to discuss the change. If no agreement is reached within the first 30 days, the parties are required to notify the Service as well as territorial or state agencies, where such exist.

After the Service becomes aware of a dispute, it must decide whether to assign the dispute to a mediator. It must be guided by the law in making this decision. However, the law is open to broad interpretation. Section 203(b) of the LMRA

The service may proffer its services in any labor dispute in any industry affecting commerce, either upon its own motion or upon the request of one or more of the parties to the dispute, whenever in its judgment such dispute threatens to cause a substantial interruption of commerce. The Director and the Service are directed to avoid attempting to mediate disputes which would have only a minor effect on interstate commerce if State or other conciliation services are available to the parties.

In interpreting this provision it seems that the Service considers the determining factor to be, not the number in the bargaining unit, but the effect of these employees on interstate commerce.

The Role of the Mediator

What happens after a mediator has been assigned to a dispute case? Normally he will contact the company and the union within a short time to ask about the status of their negotiation. If within a week of the deadline nothing has been settled, he may suggest that they all get together, offering —but not forcing—his services.

What does a mediator, who is not empowered with any legal force, do in a negotiation? He uses the quasi power of moral suasion. The effective mediator is impartial but not necessarily neutral.

46

He is not a mere badminton bird to be knocked back and forth between the parties, but rather a fearless eagle demanding and receiving respect. He tells the parties when he thinks a proposal is completely out of line, and when the situation dictates, he offers positive leadership.

In an informational pamphlet the FMCS says, "The mediator's job is *not to decide issues,* but to help the parties reconcile any differences which may exist between them." The mediator, like the orchestra leader, has players capable of discord or harmony, and the outcome of the symphony is largely dependent upon his conducting.

Private versus Joint Meetings. The mediation session normally consists of a series of private and joint meetings, with the mediator trying to help the parties narrow their differences and finally reach agreement.

In the private meetings the mediator talks freely with negotiators and tries to find out what their positions are. Having determined this, he is in a position to seek a common ground for accommodation. Usually, these private sessions, with the mediator working back and forth between the parties, are the source of the mediator's most fruitful results.

When the joint session is in progress, the mediator generally lets the parties present their positions. He tries to get all the issues out on the table. Having done this, he can decide on his course of action.

At joint meetings each side frequently presents its position with great passion. Charges and coun-

tercharges are made, tempers begin to fray, and issues supposedly settled begin to be reintroduced.
Merely keeping tempers down and minds open is
in itself an ambitious undertaking. It is no wonder
that the mediator often finds it practically impossible to get agreement in a face-to-face meeting.

For a mediator to be effective, he must retain
the confidence of the union and management
negotiators. But simply having their confidence is
not enough. Unless they give him something to
work with, he cannot be effective.

A critical time in any negotiations occurs when
both parties take positions from which they determine not to move and from which someone must
move if there is eventually to be agreement. In this
situation both parties generally recognize the value
of the mediator in providing a way for both sides to
save face and continue with bargaining.

With the mediator on the scene, the union representatives can go back and tell their membership
that a government representative is now in the picture and that previous positions may have to be altered. The management representatives can go to
their superiors and say the same. Either or both
sides can use the mediator for a scapegoat and save
face. Both parties to the negotiation know beforehand that they will probably have to do some
compromising for the mediator.

A mediator's actions are dictated by the particular situation. There are no hard and fast rules. The
role of the mediator is a rather vague and mysteri-
ous one. As Peter Seitz has observed:

As well ask a doctor how he cures the sick as ask a successful mediator how he works. Frequently, although flushed with success and satisfied with a job well done, he doesn't have the vaguest idea as to how it all came about. If he is sincere and brutally truthful with himself, he may admit that he does not know whether he was the moving cause of agreement or whether agreement was reached despite his efforts.[21]

And even those who would give the mediator more credit than Mr. Seitz does would concede that at best he is practicing not a science but a difficult art. Arthur S. Meyer has put it this way:

The sea that he sailed in is only roughly charted and its changing contours are not clearly discernible. Worse still, he has no science of navigation, no fund inherited from the experience of others. He is a solitary artist recognizing, at most, a few guiding stars and depending mainly on his personal power of divination.[22]

Mediation versus Arbitration

The functions of mediation and arbitration should not be confused or considered interchangeable. They are as separate and distinct as their objectives. When it comes to dispute resolution, the mediator is amoral and disregards the contract. His efforts are the products of mixed considerations: the economic and the political, the measurable and the immeasurable, the rational and the irrational. Like bargaining, mediation often defies logic. In mediation, grievances are settled rather than determined. As in bargaining, one thing can be traded for another and accommodation and compromise are the bywords.

Unlike the mediator, the arbitrator knows that the parties before him have chosen the peaceful uncertainty of an arbitral settlement as preferable to the costs and risks of enlarging an agreement or tampering with its contents. The arbitrator leaves the flexibility of bargaining to the mediator and instead derives his authority and usefulness from the labor contract.

Mediation: Substitute or Supplement? It is true that in a relatively few agreements the terminal point of the grievance procedure is not arbitration but mediation (by an impartial agency such as the FMCS or a state mediation service). Some other agreements offer a choice between mediation and arbitration as the last step in the procedure. In still others, mediation is an intermediate step prior to arbitration, and some of these provide that mediation may be omitted and arbitration immediately invoked by mutual consent. A few agreements provide for mediation only on nonarbitrable issues.

One clause which provided for mediation as a condition precedent to arbitration reads as follows:

In the event that the employer and the union fail to adjust a grievance arising under this grievance procedure the parties, before resorting to the arbitration procedure provided in this agreement, mutually agree to request the services of governmental conciliation, mediation, or other appropriate Government agency in an effort to settle such grievance. In the event that the grievance is not settled through the aid of such conciliation or media-

tion, any further proceedings shall be dealt with in accordance with the provisions of [the] Article [dealing
with] Arbitration.

Anderson Electric Co./Machinists (IAM)

It should be noted that the parties here have
separated the process of searching for mutual accommodation (mediation) from that in which a final
and binding conclusion is rendered (arbitration).

The Arbitrator as Mediator. Some arbitrators
feel that, by acting as mediators, they could make
enduring contributions to relations between management and labor by helping them to solve inar-
bitrable problems. Others believe that the role of
an arbitrator offers too few satisfactions unless
there is a chance for service beyond the mere calling of balls and strikes. Such arbitrators are
doomed to almost perpetual frustration, however,
since only occasionally is an arbitrator able to
mediate a dispute.

An arbitrator can act as a mediator only when
he is authorized to do so by *both* parties. The following contractual clause provides a good example
of how the parties, by mutual consent (during the
making of the contract), can permit the arbitrator to
wear two hats:

Whenever either party concludes that further conferences in the procedure set forth in Step 4 cannot settle
the grievance such party may, not later than ten (10)
days from the date of the last Step 4 meeting on the
grievance, refer the grievance to the New York State
Board of Mediation hereinafter referred to as the board.

This reference shall be in writing and shall be served upon the board and the other party. Upon receipt of such reference the board shall appoint an arbitrator to act upon the grievance. The arbitrator shall first try to mediate the grievance, but if this cannot be done, he shall arbitrate the grievance.

Sherwood Medical, Inc./United Steelworkers of America

This is a clause infrequently found. The vast majority of contracts *do not* make provision for any form of mediation within the grievance procedure. Those which do, separate the mediation function and the principal performing it, from the arbitration function and the neutral performing it; seldom are the functions commingled, as in the clause cited. And even there, where the parties want the same informed third party to participate with them in both functions to resolve their differences, they have segregated his mediation duty from his arbitration duty.

As Arbitrator Marion Beatty has stated in one of his many published decisions: "In grievance arbitrations, arbitrators are employed to interpret contracts, not to write them, add to them or modify them. If they are to be modified, that has to be done at the bargaining table. . . ." [23]

Most employers, and unions as well, would subscribe to that philosophy as it is applicable to attempts at mediation by arbiters. From the point of view of the employer, mediation by an arbitrator undermines the prevailing labor agreement and has an adverse effect on collective bargaining.

When disputes arise during the course of a collectively bargained agreement, the only question is whether the employer's action or inaction violated the provisions of that agreement. If the parties can come to some mutually satisfactory settlement of the issue within the grievance machinery, before the arbitrator enters the picture, that is well and good. But having failed in that regard and having summoned their outside neutral, they are then seeking and are entitled to a final decision which puts to an end their haggling and compromising on that issue.

A proper conception of the arbitrator's function is basic. He is not a public tribunal which is imposed upon the parties by superior authority and which they are obliged to accept. He has no general charter to administer justice for a community which transcends the parties. He is rather a part of a system of self-government created by and confined to the parties. He serves at their pleasure only, to administer the rule of law established by their collective agreement. They are entitled to demand that, at least on balance, his performance be satisfactory to them.

To the extent that an arbitrator has been guilty of improperly enlarging the scope of his jurisdiction, he must assume the appropriate blame. The arbitration mechanism is solely the creation of the parties and can be tailored to their purpose. If either party considers a particular arbitrator's views to be too flexible for its taste, the remedy is not to reject arbitration, but to reject the arbitrator.

3
KEY CONTRACT CLAUSES

A LABOR agreement is the end result of a bargain reached by a company and a union. As such it attempts to balance the needs and wishes of the company and its stockholders on the one hand with those of the employees and their union on the other. This does not necessarily mean that the contract always or even usually represents a *balanced* bargain between the parties. From the viewpoint of the company, it may be too restrictive with regard to the right to manage; and, from the viewpoint of the union, it may not be as liberal as desired regarding wages, benefits, and job security. In effect, then, the collective agreement is basically a series of compromises.

The elements of compromise are especially apparent in the four contract clauses which form the foundation of the collective agreement: (1) the management rights article, (2) the grievance procedure clause, (3) the arbitration clause, and (4) the no-strike clause. Although each of the four is designed to achieve a particular purpose, together they form an interrelated group, like the four sides of a square.

It is certainly safe to say that none of these four clauses alone can provide sufficient protection of managerial discretion. To paraphrase the words of Benjamin Franklin, "If they don't hang together, they will surely hang separately." Among the important questions such clauses must provide answers to are the following:

How are management's rights defined, and what are its limitations?

What is the definition of a grievance? What is eligible or ineligible to be considered a grievance?

What can be arbitrated, and what is nonarbitrable?

What are the limitations on the arbitrator's powers and authority?

What is the breadth and scope of the no-strike provision? Are there matters not subject to arbitration review? When such matters are in contention, will they render the no-strike provision inoperable?

To what extent do the parties intend their arbitration system to substitute for the use of economic force as a means of settling differences during the contract term?

To what extent do they expect their arbitration system to help them in self-regulating their affairs and to secure continuity of relations and uninterrupted production and jobs during the contract term?

Clearly, these are questions of basic interest which only the parties themselves can answer. Only a design of the four clauses which results in their operating complementarily will provide an answer satisfactory to management and also, perhaps, to the labor organization. The remarks of a nationally known arbitrator and labor relations consultant are relevant here:

. . . I suggest it is because the parties in many cases have not had a "meeting of the minds" on these basic questions that many of the problems of arbitrability and arbitrator's jurisdiction arise—for the parties as well as for the arbitrator.

"Any grievance or dispute arising during the term of this Agreement between the company and the union or between the company and any employees covered by this Agreement, if not settled by the Parties, shall be submitted to final and binding arbitration."

Is it not reasonable to assume that those parties intended their private arbitration system to be equivalent—coextensive—with the "no-strike–no-lockout" clause or concept, expressed or implied in their contract? And is it not equally reasonable to find that, under the clear and unambiguous language of such a clause, they intended "any grievance"—whether or not covered by a contract clause—to be arbitrable?—and to give the arbitrator serving under such a clause jurisdiction to decide "any dispute" that the parties themselves were unable to settle? We are not concerned here with the standards or guideposts that the arbitrator under such a clause would follow in deciding the merits of the dispute, but only with the question whether he would have jurisdiction to decide it. . . .[24]

We will next examine each of the four key contractual clauses separately, while attempting to reveal further how they are interrelated. The management rights article, the grievance procedure clause, and the arbitration clause will be discussed in this chapter, and the no-strike clause in Chapter 4. As we progress it will become more and more apparent that the statements on the implications of the four clauses represent the opinions and conclusions of the author and a sampling of experts. It will become readily apparent that there are no absolutely clear answers to many of the questions raised, and that, in the final analysis, any answers must be supplied by the parties themselves.

In effect, as to providing answers, the author finds himself in much the same situation as the farmer who took his young son to the big city for the first time. "Pa," the boy asked, "what are all those little clocks for on the posts at the edge of the sidewalk?" The farmer didn't rightly know. The boy then asked why the lights on tall poles were flashing red, yellow, and green in sequence, and Pa was again stymied.

Later, in front of an elevator, the boy asked, "Why do those people get in that little room and the door shuts by itself and when it opens the people are gone?" Pa couldn't rightly say. Maybe it was a magic room for making people disappear.

Finally, when the boy asked if Pa minded all those questions, the latter replied, "Why of course not, son. If you don't ask questions, how you ever gonna learn?"

It is perhaps with the same assurance that the author will now forge onward.

THE MANAGEMENT RIGHTS ARTICLE

When a union or an employee challenges an action taken by the employer, the challenge typically takes this form: "Show us (or me) where in the contract it gives you the right to do what you did." To this, management typically replies: "No, you show us where in the contract the language prohibits or restricts our right to do what we did." That reply is the essence of the theory of *residual rights,* which is the basis for all management rights articles.

This theory holds that the company retains all managerial rights (prerogatives, functions, etc.) that it has not surrendered to the union in the collective bargaining process. In other words, the contract contains specific restrictions on the functions that management would be free to exercise fully if a union were not on the premises.

According to the residual rights theory, therefore, collective bargaining is generally an attempt by the union to persuade the company to accept further contractual limitations on the exercise of its managerial functions. If it succeeds, the union obtains obvious reciprocal benefits: To the extent that management agrees to limit its own functions, those functions are no longer within the province of its authority or control. Such matters are then beyond its power to alter, modify, or reduce.[25]

Although management rights clauses are based on residual rights, they vary widely both in form and substance. One reason for this is that the needs, requirements, and problems of different industries are so dissimilar. For example, in some industries it is essential that standards of production be determined by management and not be subject to review in the grievance procedure or by arbitration. In other industries, such a normally vital function as the establishment of piece rates may be delegated to the union. It is clear then that what is regarded as an essential management right in one industry may be willingly bargained away in another.

Management rights articles also vary with the particular viewpoint of the company or its labor relations representative. Some employers favor a clause which includes a list of the specific prerogatives of management. Others advocate a much shorter clause, stated in broad terms, while still others prefer to dispense with the management rights clause altogether.

Those employers who favor an enumerated statement clearly defining the rights of management believe it offers better protection against erosion. Those who prefer a general clause, which is essentially a restatement of the residual rights principle, argue that any list of the specific prerogatives of management may omit important ones inadvertently and thus impair their effectiveness.

The third group of employers goes one step further. They consider management rights clauses unnecessary on the grounds that the residual rights principle exists outside of the contract and protects all functions not specifically abridged by the terms of the agreement. In their view, to affirm their residual rights in the contract is to restate the obvious and to enumerate their rights is not only unnecessary but downright dangerous. In other words, they not only subscribe to the residual rights concept, they choose to put *all* their faith in its support.

The following is an example of the enumerated type of management rights clause. This rather lengthy version might be titled the A-to-Z model:

Section 5—Rights of Management

Except as otherwise specifically provided in this Agreement, the Employer has the sole and exclusive right to exercise all the rights or functions of management, and the exercise of any such rights or functions shall not be subject to the grievance or arbitration provisions of this Agreement.

Without limiting the generality of the foregoing, as used herein, the term "Rights of Management" includes:
- (a) The right to manage the plant.
- (b) The right to schedule working hours.
- (c) The right to establish, modify or change work schedules or standards.
- (d) The right to direct the working forces, including the right to hire, promote or transfer any employee.
- (e) The location of the business, including the estab-

lishment of new plants or departments, divisions or subdivisions thereof, and the relocation or closing of plants, departments, divisions or subdivisions thereof.

(f) The determination of products to be manufactured or sold or services to be rendered or supplied.

(g) The determination of the layout and the machinery, equipment or materials to be used in the business.

(h) The determination of processes, techniques, methods and means of manufacture, maintenance or distribution, including any changes or adjustments of any machinery or equipment.

(i) The determination of the size and character of inventories.

(j) The determination of financial policy, including accounting procedures, prices of goods or services rendered or supplied, and customer relations.

(k) The determination of the organization of each production, service, maintenance, or distribution department, division or subdivision or any other production, maintenance, service or distribution unit deemed appropriate by the employer.

(l) The selection, promotion, or transfer of employees to supervisory or other managerial positions or to positions outside of the bargaining unit.

(m) The determination of the size of the working force.

(n) The allocation and assignment of work to employees.

(o) The determination of policy affecting the selection or training of new employees.

(p) The establishment of quality and quantity standards and the judgment of the quality and quantity of workmanship required.

(q) The control and use of operations and the determination of the number and duration of shifts.

(r) The scheduling of operations and the determination of the number and duration of the shifts.

(s) The determination of safety, health and property protection measures for the plants.

(t) The establishment, modification and enforcement of reasonable plant rules or regulations, which are not in direct conflict with any other provisions of this Agreement.

(u) The transfer of work from one job to another or from one plant, department, division or other plant unit to another.

(v) Introduction of new, improved or different production, maintenance, service or distribution methods or facilities or a change in existing methods or facilities.

(w) The placing of production, service, maintenance or distribution work with outside contractors or subcontractors.

(x) The determination of the amount of supervision necessary.

(y) The right to terminate, merge or sell the business or any part thereof.

(z) The transfer of employees from one job to another or from one department, division or other plant unit to another.

Samsonite Corporation/United Rubber Workers Union

The following example of a general statement of management rights offers an obvious contrast to the A-to-Z model:

The Union and the Locals recognize that subject only to the express provisions of this Agreement, the supervision, management, and control of the Company's business operations and plants are exclusively the function of the Company.

General Electric Company/International Brotherhood of Electrical Workers

Here is another general statement, which, like the A-to-Z model, was negotiated by the United Rubber Workers. Obviously, this union has agreed to both types of management rights clauses.

The Management of the business and the operation of the plants and the authority to execute all the various duties, functions and responsibilities incident thereto is vested in the Employer. The exercise of such authority shall not conflict with this Agreement, its purposes, or the supplements thereto.

Goodyear Tire & Rubber Company/United Rubber Workers Union (expires April, 1976)

Regardless of their differences in form or approach, the three examples above—and, for that matter, any other management rights articles —clearly indicate that the essence of the management functions is the *exclusive power to initiate action.* The union cannot direct its members to their work stations or work assignments, or tell them to go home because there is no work. The union does not discipline or discharge employees for work-rule violations, nor can it notify people who are discharged to stay on the job. The union does not tell employees to report for work at the end of a layoff. It does not start or stop operations.

In other words, the company, not the union, is primarily the party which decides and acts. As a labor relations maxim puts it, "The company acts; the union reacts."

How the employer acts is determined, at least in part, by the management rights clause. How the union or individual employees react initially to those company actions with which they disagree is determined by the contractual grievance procedure.

THE GRIEVANCE PROCEDURE

The industrial plant is a dynamic community in which changes frequently occur: Job and work situations may be altered from time to time, and decisions are made and actions taken that are not always agreeable to all employees. The enterprise requires the continuous coordination of the work of employees, perhaps multitudes of employees, and this poses numerous daily problems. So elementary a matter as leaving the job for a few minutes poses a serious problem which must be carefully analyzed and provided for; otherwise, the work of a hundred men might conceivably be held up every time one of them had to leave.

Every day a number of employees may be absent or late. Daily or almost daily some employees may have to be laid off or hired and changes must be made in job assignments, either by way of promotion or demotion or otherwise. And daily there may be occasions for friction between the employee and the supervisor.

When differences of opinion occur between management representatives and employees or union officials, it is unfortunately not uncommon for the employee (or the union) to retaliate by resorting to self-help. Such a tactic may manifest itself in any of various forms: Production output may be controlled and reduced, or standards of quality lowered or disregarded; industrial sabotage might occur, with machines and other equipment mysteriously malfunctioning; or the employees may totally withhold their productive effort by walking out, sitting down, or staying away.

The grievance and arbitration procedures can prevent such "labor fires." When the plant's labor relations get so hot that a flare-up is going to break out, that is the time for responsible labor and management firemen to cool them off with the grievance machinery extinguishers. When an illegal work stoppage threatens, such grievance processes should be offered with the assurance they will be instantly implemented and, in good faith, carried forth.

It is hard for reasoning men to justify industrial warfare under any circumstances, but even less excuse can be found where the fighting parties have taken the trouble to set up a grievance-arbitration process for the purpose of avoiding such destructive confrontations.

The Advantages

The establishment and regulation of a grievance procedure is a major union objective in collective bargaining. The chief reason for the grievance provisions in a labor agreement is to provide employees and the union with a mechanism by which they can raise and resolve their disagreements with the employer. In other words, the grievance machinery is intended to provide a formal, orderly means for raising and processing a claim alleging a contract violation by the company. Because management is generally the party which decides and acts, labor agreements seldom provide it with the right to file a grievance.

However, despite its obvious benefits to the union and employees, the grievance procedure should not be construed as being anti-employer. On the contrary, it offers the company several benefits. For example, when a collective agreement includes provisions for a grievance procedure and for arbitration, the union has an implied obligation not to strike during the term of the agreement.[26]

Another benefit to the company, and to the union as well, is the fact that the grievance procedure is a key part of the problem-solving, dispute-settling machinery of the labor agreement. It is the first stage in an attempt by both parties to resolve their differences in a peaceful, orderly, and expeditious manner. If it should fail, it usually sets into motion the second stage, arbitration. Thus, the grievance mechanism permits the company and the union to investigate and discuss their problems sensibly and amicably, and to resolve them fairly, without the need for either party to resort to economic force or to interrupt business operations.

In a recent BNA study, virtually all (99 percent) of the labor agreements surveyed included a procedure for handling grievances. In 94 percent of the sample, the terminal point in the grievance process was arbitration.

The actual method of handling the complaint varied considerably among the agreements analyzed and reflected different plant and company organizational or decision-making structures. The size of the plant or company was the key factor; that is, the larger the unit, the more formalized the grievance procedure tended to become.

A few contracts described the grievance procedure in a general, informal way, but most were more detailed, listing the procedural steps through which a dispute would be processed if agreement was not reached. Some highly formal provisions included as many as six or more steps, but three or four steps were most common.[27]

This discussion will now focus on the experience and attitudes of a major manufacturer (General Motors) and a major union in another industry (United Steelworkers of America) in an attempt to examine problems which can undermine the grievance process and their possible solution.

The Problems

The following is part of the General Motors management's prepared statement to the United Auto Workers Union on July 26, 1973, at the commencement of their bargaining for a renewal contract:

Grievance and Representation Procedure—The grievance procedure and representation provisions are at the heart of the relationship between employees, the union and the company. An orderly procedure to insure the prompt and fair handling of employee complaints without costly disruptions in production and employee earnings is of paramount interest to all of the parties to the collective bargaining relationship.

The employee is entitled to a prompt and fair disposition of his complaint based on the facts and merits of the case. The company is entitled to an orderly procedure without continual disruptions of the production process. And an orderly and expeditious grievance procedure is also an essential interest of the union in the performance of its duty to represent its members fairly.

The GM-UAW grievance and umpire procedure has historically been considered one of the finest in U.S. industry. It has served as a model for many other companies and unions. However, in recent years a number of problems and unfavorable trends have developed which have caused the procedure to be undermined at a number of locations. If these unfavorable trends are permitted by the parties to continue, the entire procedure will break down and employees will increasingly search out other forums available to them for pursuing their complaints.

In the past ten years, the number of written grievances has nearly doubled from 138,000 in 1963 to 264,000 in 1972. This 91 per cent increase in grievances was far greater than the 15 per cent increase in employment during the same period. A high percentage of these grievances are concentrated in a growing group of plants where literally thousands of grievances are written and allowed to pile up with little effort made to re-solve them promptly on their merits. Instead, they are accumulated, a crisis situation is precipitated, and then a demand is made to settle them on a wholesale basis with little or no regard to the facts or merits. A deterio-ration of the grievance procedure is clearly not in the mutual interest of employees, the union or the corpora-tion.

In the corporation's opinion, it would be helpful in achieving our mutual goal if committeemen would dis-cuss employee's complaints and try to resolve them *verbally* with supervision *before* a grievance is reduced to writing and presented to management. Such discus-sion, in many instances, could profitably include the General Foreman and even higher supervision. Many problems and complaints could be satisfactorily re-solved in this way, but if they were not, the right to file a grievance with the foreman would still be preserved. The Corporation proposes that we discuss and reach agreement on this desirable implementation of our formal grievance procedure.

There has been a growing tendency on the part of some employees to resort to various forums in an effort to seek redress for grievances real or imaginary. This has been a growing concern of both parties. It is a matter of concern because it disregards the time-tested proce-dures of the National Agreement. More than that, it sub-stitutes other forums for the one under which em-ployees are represented by their duly authorized col-lective bargaining agent.

Perhaps the area of charges of discrimination is the one in which this most often occurs. It may be that Para-graph (6a) should be modified so that recourse to the grievance procedure will be attractive in legitimate cases without the burden of documenting in writing support for the charge, as is presently required.

At the same time the grievance form should include a space where the employee could specify whether or not he was claiming that the action protested was a violation of Paragraph (6a). This would tend to encourage employees to utilize the grievance procedure for the resolution of discrimination grievances. It would also establish at the point when the grievance was filed whether the employee did or did not contend that he had been discriminated against.

Every effort should be made by the parties to resolve Paragraph (6a) cases at the earliest step of the procedure following a thorough investigation. Such early resolution, coupled with counselling of all involved parties where appropriate would, it is hoped, begin to build greater confidence on the part of the minority employee that his or her grievance will be fairly handled under the contractual procedure.

In addition, it is imperative that we take action in these negotiations to expedite the processing of grievances in the procedure. A business-like approach to the Second Step meetings *is required.* In that regard, *there can be no justification by any shop committee for not submitting a complete agenda in advance of the items to be discussed* at the forthcoming meeting.

The difficulty in scheduling and holding Third Step meetings at some locations has *long been a complaint* of General Motors. *Something must be done* in these negotiations to correct that situation by insuring that Third Step meetings are held with sufficient frequency and regularity to deal with cases appealed to that step of the procedure.

These and other matters relating to the grievance procedure will be the subject of proposals by the Corporation in these negotiations.[28]

It is refreshing and encouraging that General Motors and—it can be assumed—its UAW Union are concerned over the operation of their contractual grievance machinery. At the same time, however, this GM proposal reveals some problems in their relationship. In other settings, the problems listed below might be almost humorous. But here they were to be the subject of discussions about a national agreement involving almost half a million workers. In such a setting these problems can be viewed only as distressing if not tragic:

1. The GM-UAW grievance and umpire procedure experienced a 91 percent increase in grievances in a ten-year period in which GM employment increased by only 15 percent.

Although that point alone is startling, it takes on greater meaning in light of these facts: The two parties began their collective bargaining relationship in 1937, almost 40 years ago. One of the parties is perhaps the world's largest and most powerful industrial concern; the other is one of the world's most powerful unions. Moreover, in GM's own words, their grievance and umpire procedure "has historically been considered one of the finest in U.S. industry. It has served as a model for many other companies and unions."

2. The company found it necessary to emphasize that the union's shop committees must stop withholding from management a complete

agenda of what they wished to discuss in forthcoming meetings.

It would not be surprising to find such a problem confronting a small employer with a newly established union. That situation would involve union and management representatives unsophisticated in labor-management relations and unaccustomed to working together harmoniously. But when the problem besets parties with almost 40 years together, one can reasonably conclude that it is only a symptom of much larger, more deeply rooted employer-employee problems.

3. The company proposal urged that union committeemen try to resolve grievances orally *before* they are submitted in writing.

An oral first step is widely considered to be *fundamental* to the successful operation of a grievance procedure. In many formal setups, the first step provides for a discussion of the complaint among the foreman, the employee, and the steward before the grievance is submitted in writing. Because the dispute can often be resolved during that oral step, it is probably the most important one of the entire grievance procedure.

Yet, despite the fact that the current GM-UAW procedure called for an oral first step and despite GM's long relationship with UAW, the company found it necessary to call for greater efforts to resolve grievances orally.

4. The proposal called for faster processing of grievances.

A principal objective of the grievance machinery is the speedy resolution of disputes. Increasing employee dissatisfaction is inevitable if grievances are not settled swiftly. And even when the process is relatively fast, the interval between the employee's complaint and his receipt of the ultimate decision often is long enough to place a strain on labor relations. This need for swift justice for aggrieved workers was at the heart of the substantially revamped grievance procedure negotiated by the United Steelworkers of America during the 1971 bargaining talks. The significant procedural changes are discussed in the following subsection.

The Solution?

In its 1971 prenegotiation statement, the USWA's committee noted that the strike might be the only alternative should the grievance and arbitration system collapse. It was the union's "firm determination in forthcoming negotiations to provide a solution which will avert the need to resort to such an alternative. Such solution must be one that speeds up grievance resolution, keeps the problems close to the plants, and is inexpensive, non-technical and fair."

"At some locations," the prenegotiation statement stressed, "the grievance procedure becomes so clogged at certain times that it ceases to fulfill its vital function. . . . Mechanisms *must* be found by the parties to cope with these backlogs by assuring expeditious handling of disputes, eliminating unnecessary steps, and providing fair, efficient and less costly arbitration."

The union's "firm determination" produced many major revisions in the grievance and arbitration procedures. (The revised arbitration process will be covered later in this chapter.) Because of the importance of those changes, they were —before ratification of the agreement—reviewed in great detail to presidents of basic steel locals and at the Basic Steel Contract Briefing Conference held in Pittsburgh in late September, 1971. The agreement was ratified by the USWA Basic Steel Industry Conference in Washington on September 30.

The revisions that will be discussed here are not the only ones brought about by the 1971 agreement, but they are perhaps the most significant:

1. Interestingly, in light of the earlier GM review, in basic steel both Step 1 and Step 2 of the grievance procedure have become *oral* steps.

2. While the time limits between steps vary somewhat from company to company, all such limits insure the prompt processing of complaints through the grievance channels. No longer can much more than a month elapse, for example, in moving a complaint from Step 1 through Step 3.

3. The responsibilities of the local-union grievance officials and staff representatives have been clarified as have those of the foreman and other company representatives, and their authority to settle complaints has been spelled out.

4. Also, the foreman now has authority to settle the complaint at Step 1, and the assistant grievance committeeman has authority to settle or withdraw the complaint of the involved individual(s).

. 5. The settlement of a complaint in Step 1 or

Step 2 "shall be without prejudice to the position of either party."

6. The participation of the worker(s) and foreman involved in the complaint is now required. This step contemplates a full hearing in which all available pertinent facts are disclosed in an effort to resolve the complaint.

These developments in the basic steel grievance machinery are a hopeful sign that peaceful, prompt, and just settlement of labor-management problems is in fact possible. On the other hand, there are perhaps more-significant trends which indicate that the present state of our labor-management health is far from good: The recent poor national strike record, which was summarized in Chapter 1, and the breakdown of the grievance procedure as exemplified by the GM proposal discussed above.

In the face of such evidence can it be persuasively argued that our system of industrial relations and collective bargaining is working effectively?

However, it cannot be denied that when the grievance machinery is working effectively, it can resolve satisfactorily the overwhelming majority of disputes between the parties. Those disputes it cannot cope with can be fed into the arbitration end of the process.

The Arbitration Clause

Arbitrators and courts have called management's agreement to arbitrate grievance disputes the quid pro quo for the union's agreement not to strike.[29] In other words, in exchange for a no-strike promise from the union, management provides a contractual substitute for the strike—the grievance and arbitration procedures.

In this way, the union is provided peaceful, orderly, and expeditious processes through which it can obtain remedy and relief from improper management actions. The company gains a commitment assuring uninterrupted operations, and the union gains a means of challenging and reversing management's decisions and actions. Fortunately, a good many labor contracts contain provisions for the voluntary submission to arbitration of grievances arising during the contract's term.

Supreme Court Rulings

The development of arbitration has been shaped by three vital Supreme Court decisions concerning the interpretation and application of arbitration provisions. The Court's rulings and rationale in the three arbitration decisions, known as the "trilogy," will be briefly reviewed here:

In the first case, *Steelworkers* v. *Warrior & Gulf Navigation Company*,[30] the union sought to compel arbitration of a dispute involving the company's right to contract out major repair work. Under the labor agreement in force, matters strictly considered functions of management were not deemed to be subject to arbitration.

The district court and the court of appeals ruled in favor of the company, holding that the agreement did not give an arbitrator the right to review the employer's business judgment in contracting out work. This ruling held further that the contracting out of repair and maintenance work, as well as construction work, was strictly a function of management and therefore not limited in any respect by the labor agreement involved.

However, the Supreme Court reversed that ruling in favor of the union. The Court held the dispute arbitrable because there was no express contractual provision defining the contracting out of work as a function of management. Speaking for the majority of the Court, Justice Douglas said:

In the absence of any express provision excluding the particular grievance from arbitration, we think only the most forceful evidence of a purpose to exclude the claim from arbitration can prevail, particularly where, as here, the exclusion clause is vague and the arbitration clause quite broad.

In the second case, *Steelworkers* v. *American Manufacturing Company*,[31] the union sued to compel arbitration of a dispute involving a member's seniority rights. The union claimed that the company violated the collectively bargained contract's seniority provisions by refusing to reinstate an employee who had left his job because of injuries and had settled a workman's compensation claim against the company for his permanent partial disability.

The employer refused to arbitrate on the ground that the dispute was not arbitrable under the contract. The lower court and the court of appeals upheld that view and ruled that the union member was prevented from claiming any seniority or employment rights. Furthermore, they called the grievance frivolous and patently baseless.

In reversing, the Supreme Court referred to the relevant arbitration provision in the agreement which points out that any disputes arising between the parties as to the "meaning, interpretation and application of the contract" may be submitted to arbitration. In its decision the Court gave great weight to law review articles by Harvard Professor Archibald Cox, who said: " . . . it seems proper to read the typical arbitration clause as a promise to arbitrate every clause, meritorious or frivolous, which the complainant bases upon the contract."

The third case, *Steelworkers* v. *Enterprise Wheel & Car Corporation*,[32] involved the merits of an arbitrator's award directing the employer to reinstate certain discharged employees and to pay them back-wages for periods both before and after expiration of the contract. When the company refused to comply, the union petitioned for enforcement of the award.

The trial court sustained the arbitrator but its ruling was reversed by the court of appeals, which held that the order for reinstatement of the discharged employees was unenforceable because the contract had expired. However, the Supreme Court reversed the appeals court and ordered full enforcement. In upholding the arbitrator's award, Justice Douglas declared in the majority opinion:

Interpretation of the collective bargaining agreement is a question for the arbitrator. It is the arbitrator's construction which was bargained for; and so far as the arbitrator's decision concerns construction of the contract, the courts have no business overruling him because their interpretation of the contract is different from his.

In these three decisions, the Supreme Court limited the role of the courts in collective bargaining arbitration cases. That role now largely became one of determining: (1) whether the claim of one of the parties is governed by the contract (not whether it has merit); (2) whether the contractual arbitration clause covers the dispute (if the dispute is *not clearly excluded* from arbitration, the courts should send the case to the arbitrator); and (3) whether the arbitrator based his award on the contract and remained within his authority (if he did, the court may not overrule him even though it disagrees with his award).

Types of Arbitration Clauses

Arbitration clauses can be broadly divided into two classes: the general and the specific. The specific clause is often the result of the employer's attempt to ameliorate the effects of the Supreme Court trilogy by reforming a general clause. The following is a typical general clause:

Any dispute arising under the terms of this Agreement which cannot be settled between the parties involved may be submitted by either party on written notice to the other party, to an arbitration committee for their determination.

Dravo-Doyle Co./Operating Engineers

An example of a specific clause is given below. This clause, provided and recommended by a special subcommittee on arbitration of the Chamber of Commerce of the United States, clearly reflects an attempt to protect the company's powers by circumscribing those of the arbitrator:

The arbitrator shall be empowered except as his powers are limited below, to make a decision in cases of alleged violation of rights expressly accorded by this Agreement or written local agreements supplementary thereto. The limitations on the powers of the arbitrator are as follows:

(1) He shall have no power to add to, subtract from, or modify any of the terms of any agreement.

(2) He shall have no power to establish wage scales or change any wage.

(3) He shall have no discretion for the Company's discretion in cases where the Company has retained discretion or is given discretion by this Agreement or by any supplementary Agreement, except that where he finds a disciplinary layoff or discharge results from a manifestly arbitrary exercise of the Company's managerial judgment in fixing the extent of the penalty, he may make appropriate modifications of the penalty subject to (provisions concerning strike discipline).

(4) He shall have no power to (here can be recited specific matters, if any, upon which the Arbitrator may not rule) decide any question which, under this Agreement, is within the right of Management to decide. In rendering decisions, the arbitrator shall have due regard for the rights and responsibilities of Management and shall so construe the Agreement that there will be no interference with the exercise of such rights as may be expressly conditioned by the Agreement.

(5) The Company shall not be required to pay back wages prior to the date a written grievance is filed with the Company.

(6) All awards of back wages shall be limited to the amount of wages the employee would otherwise have earned from his employment with the company during the periods as above defined, less any unemployment or other compensation for personal services that he may have received from any source during the period. If the grievance is based upon a claim of violation of rights expressly accorded by this Agreement and if the dispute is one which, under this Agreement, is within the arbitrator's power to decide, the Regional Director or other representative of the International Union, by notifying the Central Industrial Relations Office of the Company in writing within____ days after disposition made pursuant to Section (the provision governing the voluntary state next preceding arbitration) of this Article of its intention to do so, may appeal the grievance to an impartial arbitrator, in accordance with and subject to the provisions of this Section.

The notice of appeal shall specify the issue raised by the grievance and shall include a statement of the nature of the grievance, together with the award requested.

Is the specific type of arbitration clause preferable to the general type? Needless to say, labor relations experts have argued that question of the "ideal" arbitration clause for years—and could continue to do so for many more years—without resolution. Rather than engage in such fruitless speculation, this discussion will now explore the manner in which some parties have actually reformed their arbitration procedures to insure labor-management peace. Two such "expedited arbitration procedures" will be reviewed—that of the General Electric Company and the International Union of Electrical Workers (IUE) and that of the United Steelworkers of America and the basic steel industry.

Expedited Arbitration Procedures

The General Electric Company and the Electrical Workers (IUE) first put an expedited arbitration procedure into effect in September, 1971, and it was subsequently extended to run concurrently with the 1973–1976 GE-IUE national agreement. The expedited arbitration agreement provides (1) for a hearing on contested discharges and upgradings to be held within 60 days of the appointment of an arbitrator and (2) for the elimination of written opinions and transcripts in certain cases.

The parties' objectives were to reduce the *cost* of arbitration and the *time* needed to process a case through arbitration. The parties said when the agreement was renewed that during the initial trial period the objectives "were more than realized." The cost of an experimental arbitration case was reduced to about half that of a regular case, and the time taken to process a case was reduced by almost six months. (For the full text of this expedited arbitration procedure, see Appendix 1.)

The expedited arbitration procedure of the United Steelworkers Union and the basic steel industry was adopted on an experimental basis as part of the 1971 basic steel contract settlement, which was discussed earlier with respect to its grievance machinery. The new arbitration process was designed to provide prompt and efficient handling of routine cases.

Under the expedited procedure, appeals to arbitration are made by the union's staff man or the local union grievance committee chairman as specified by the appropriate USWA district director. When the panel of arbitrators for any given plant is ready to function, the local parties are so informed. Arbitrators' expenses and fees are borne equally by the company and the local union, and either the company or the union can rule out the use of the arbitration process for any specific grievance at the plant level.

A grievance may be taken directly from Step 3 to arbitration (subject to the approval of the Fourth Step representative), with the appeal to arbitration being made within ten days of Step 3 (using the next listed panel member, if the designated arbitrator is not available to conduct a hearing within that limited time). An arbitrator's decision must be rendered within 48 hours after the conclusion of the hearing.

The hearings are informal. No briefs are filed or transcripts made, and there are no formal evidence rules. It is the arbitrator's obligation to have all necessary facts and considerations brought before him by the representatives of the parties. In all respects, he is to insure that the hearing is a fair one.

Any grievance appealed to the expedited arbitration system must be confined to issues which do not involve novel problems and which have limited contractual significance or complexity. If the arbitrator or the parties conclude at the hearing that the issues are complex or significant enough to require further consideration by the parties, the case is referred to the Fourth Step and processed as though appealed to the Fourth Step on the date of the arbitral hearing.

The arbitrator's decision in this expedited procedure is based on the record developed by the parties before and at the hearing and includes a brief written explanation of the basis for his conclusion. However, such a decision may not be cited as a precedent in any discussion of grievances at any step of the grievance or arbitration procedures. (For the full text of this expedited arbitration procedure, see Appendix 2.)

This review has now explored three of the essential clauses in the labor-management agreement. It is now time to "sketch" the fourth side of the square, the no-strike clause.

4
THE NO-STRIKE PLEDGE

THE BASIC promise a union can give to an employer in return for the many promises it receives in a labor agreement is that there will be no strikes during the term of the agreement. Unless this single no-strike promise flows from the bargaining agent to the employer, the latter does not consider the labor contract a true bilateral agreement. The importance of the explicit no-strike commitment to the employer is borne out by a BNA study which indicates that it is contained in more than 94 percent of labor contracts.[33]

The no-strike pledge enables an employer to make plans. Commitments can be made and deliveries scheduled on the assumption of uninterrupted production for the period of the contract. Obviously, the overwhelming majority of employers view the no-strike clause, standing alone, as the contractual provision of the utmost importance to them. In fact they consider it to be the only meaningful promise they derive from the contents of their labor contract.

When work stoppages occur in breach of this agreement, the union is unlawfully resorting to the use of those economic forces that presumably had been deactivated, at least for the term of the contract. Management is thereby denied the sole consideration it bargained for, and the economic purpose of the agreement—the guarantee of uninterrupted operations—is frustrated.[34]

TYPES OF NO-STRIKE CLAUSES

No-strike promises vary substantially in phraseology and substance but generally fall into one of two categories, unconditional and conditional. Unconditional pledges prohibit any form of strike, slowdown, or work stoppage during the term of the collective bargaining agreement. In conditional pledges the no-strike condition may be lifted under certain circumstances prescribed in the contract, for example, when the grievance procedure is exhausted, or perhaps when an arbitration award has not been complied with.

The Unconditional No-Strike Pledge

This type of contractual promise appears in more than three-quarters of the labor agreements in the leather, rubber, paper, utility, maritime, insurance and finance, and stone industries. It also appears in half of the agreements in the chemicals, fabricated metals, food, lumber, machinery, primary metals, petroleum, textiles services, and retail and wholesale fields.[35]

Some examples of this unconditional type of ban on strikes will follow. The first is a rather lengthy provision:

Section 32—Strikes, Lockouts and Boycotts.
(a) During the term of this Agreement or during any extension or renewal thereof, neither the union nor its members, agents, representatives or confederates, or any person acting in concert with them, will cause, sanction, or take part in any strike, walkout, picketing, stoppage of work, retarding of work, boycott (whether of a primary or secondary nature) or any other interference with the operations or conduct of the Employer's business.

(b) During the term of this Agreement, or any extension or renewal thereof, neither the union nor its members, agents, representatives or confederates, or any person acting in concert with them, will engage in any form of economic pressure by publications, advertisements, or otherwise directed against the Employer, its owners or managers, or the products or services of the Employer.

(c) During the term of this Agreement or during any extension or renewal thereof, the Union will not place the Employer or the Employer's products or services on any "We do not patronize" or unfair lists, or request any other labor organization or group, association, council or federation of labor organizations, to place the Employer or the Employer's products or services on any "We do not patronize" or unfair lists.

(d) Violation of any provision of this Section 32 by the Union shall be cause for the Employer's terminating this Agreement upon the giving of a written notice to this effect to the President of Local 779 and the President of the International Union, in addition to whatever other remedies may be available to the Employer at law or in equity.

(e) For the purposes of this Section 32, acts by employees of the Employer (who are not officers of Local 779 or of the International Union) which are not authorized or acquiesced in by the Union shall not be deemed acts of the Union.

(f) Violation of any of the provisions of this Section 32 by any employee of the Employer shall be just cause for the immediate discharge of that employee. If the Employer discharges or otherwise disciplines any employee for taking part in a strike, walkout, picketing, stoppage of work, retarding of work, boycott, or any other interference with the operation or conduct of the Employer's business, only the question of fact as to whether the employee took part in a strike, walkout, picketing, stoppage of work, retarding of work, boycott, or any other interference with the operation or conduct of the Employer's business shall be subject to review through the grievance or arbitration procedure of this Agreement.

(g) During the term of this Agreement or any extensions or renewals thereof, there shall be no lockouts by the Employer. Violation of the provisions of this paragraph (g) by the Employer shall be cause for the Union's immediately terminating this Agreement, upon the giving of written notice to this effect to the Employer's Director of Industrial Relations, in addition to whatever other remedies may be available to the Union at law or in equity.

Samsonite Corporation/United Rubber Workers, Local 779 (1971–1974)

Note that paragraph (g) includes the no-lockout pledge of the company as an integral part of the union's no-strike promise. (The appearance of no-lockout pledges in collective contracts seems to be almost as frequent as that of no-strike pledges. In fact, a BNA study found no-lockout pledges in 81 percent of its sample, and these provisions contained conditions similar to, if not the same as, those found in no-strike clauses.) [36]

Note also the somewhat untypical penalties for violations of either the no-strike (d) or the no-lockout (g) conditions. Many parties to labor-management contracts—and certainly most unions—would view the termination of the contractual relationship as a penalty for such violations as unreasonable, and perhaps even unrealistic.

Much more typical of no-strike articles, however, is paragraph (f), in which an employee who violates the no-strike pledge is subject to immediate discharge or other discipline and only the question of his involvement is to be decided by an arbitrator or through established grievance procedures.

Note that penalties for breach of the no-strike promise may be directed against the union or individual employees (or both). Presumably, by spelling out in the contract specific penalties for no-strike violations, an employer will cause potential offenders to think twice about engaging in such activities. Contractual penalties are of course negotiated by the parties themselves and may not preclude actions for damages provided for in the Taft Act (see Chapter 4).

It should prove interesting to compare the substance and phrasing of the foregoing clause with a few other unconditional no-strike pledges, such as this one:

During the term of this Agreement neither the Union nor any employee shall (a) engage in or in any way encourage or sanction any strike or other action which shall interrupt or interfere with work or production at any of the plants or (b) prevent or attempt to prevent the access of employees to any of the plants. During the term of this Agreement the company shall not engage in any lockout of employees at any of the plants.

Bethlehem Steel Company/United Steelworkers of America (expired August, 1974)

The next example places emphasis on strike prevention:

The Union and its official representatives will take every reasonable precaution to prevent any threat of, preparation for, or any unauthorized work stoppage, walkout or strike.

A&P, Acme, and Food Fair Stores/Teamsters Union (expired March, 1973)

An interesting question on that provision might be whether the parties to the contract would interpret the phrase "every reasonable precaution" in the same way.

The following example is interesting primarily for its brevity:

There shall be no strike, work stoppages or interruption or impeding of work. No officer or representatives of the

Union shall authorize, instigate and/or condone any such activities. No employee shall participate in any such activities.

Jones & Laughlin Steel Corporation/United Steelworkers of America (expired August, 1974)

The Conditional No-Strike Pledge

Probably the majority of employers view conditional pledges as inadequate insurance against the disruption of operations. But, for the most part, a labor contract's provisions constitute a compromise of the most desired objectives of each party, and the no-strike clause is no exception. Perhaps some companies are satisfied with conditional no-strike assurances, but many more would prefer the unconditional type if it were obtainable.

The BNA study mentioned earlier found that over 80 percent of conditional no-strike provisions stated that the international union must approve the strike and almost 50 percent specified who might or might not call a strike. In addition, 87 percent of the clauses required the union to order a resumption of work, and 53 percent required it to make a public disavowal of the stoppage.

The BNA study also indicated the following circumstances under which a contract may permit the no-strike ban to be lifted (the figure in parentheses indicates the percentage of surveyed contracts in which that condition was prescribed):

Failure of the grievance procedure to resolve the dispute (30 percent).

A violation of an arbitration award (30 percent).

Refusal by the company to arbitrate a dispute (16 percent).

A deadlocked contract reopener (10 percent).

Other issues outside the scope of the grievance and arbitration procedure (21 percent). These clauses appeared chiefly in contracts of the transportation industry and most often concerned disputes over production standards.

Some contracts permit a strike after mediation efforts have failed (in agreements where arbitration is not prescribed as the final recourse) or after a specified cooling-off period. The clauses that follow contain a mere few of the many reasons for suspending the no-strike pledge that can be found in collective bargaining agreements:

Pending the settlement of any issue or grievance between the parties, there shall be no lockouts, strikes or work stoppages by either party. Any employee or employees who engage in unauthorized work stoppages shall be subject to discharge.

The provisions of this Section shall not be effective if (1) either party fails to abide by the Grievance Adjustment and Arbitration provision of this agreement, or (2) there is failure of the parties to reach agreement pursuant to the reopening provision of this Agreement.

FMC Corporation, San Jose Division/International Association of Machinists

In other words, the no-strike pledge can be suspended for failure to abide by the grievance and arbitration provision or to reach agreement on a wage reopener. However, the reader may wonder what failure within the grievance machinery would be sufficient to lift the no-strike ban. Also, would the parties to the contract agree in their interpretation of the meaning and intent of the clause?

The following clause seeks to insure that the company will not refuse to arbitrate, and that it will honor the arbitrator's award.

The Union will not call or sanction any strike, work stoppage, slowdown, interruption or delay of work of any nature during the terms of this Agreement except for (1) the Company's failure to abide by the Arbitration Clause of this Agreement, or (2) the Company's failure to comply with any decision of any Board of Arbitration established hereunder within ten (10) work days after such decision is received by the Company.

Marion Power Shovel Company, Inc./International Association of Machinists (expired March, 1975)

The next example deals with procedures to be followed to permit suspension of the pledge not to strike.

With respect to any grievance relating to new wage rates, production standards, or safety and health which is not settled in the Step 4 meeting, the Grievance Procedure will be deemed to have been exhausted following receipt by the Union of the final company statement of position. . . . Following such exhaustion of the Grievance Procedure if the Union determines that the grievance shall be subject to strike action, written notice of such Union decision shall be given to the Company by the authorized representative of the Union. From the date such written notice of the Union's action is given to the Company there shall be a ten (10) working day period during which there shall be no strike or other interference with or interruption of production. The Company and the Union shall make every effort during this ten (10) working day period to settle the grievance to prevent a strike or lockout. Moreover, in any event, there shall be no strike action unless and until such action has been fully authorized as provided in the Constitution of the International Union AIW, AFL-CIO.

Clark Equipment Company, Transmission Division/Allied Industrial Workers Union

The suspension of the no-strike assurance here occurs only upon proper authorization by the international union.

The example below requires a 45-day notice before the union can strike and nullifies the right to strike if the union has not acted within the next 45 days.

There shall be no strikes, work stoppages or interruption or impeding of work, except, however, the Union shall have the right to strike only concerning the earnings opportunity presented by a new incentive rate or the rate for a new day work classification and only after strict compliance on the part of the Union with the following procedure . . . No such strike shall begin until forty-five (45) days following the receipt by the Company of such notices. During this period or any mutually agreed upon extension thereof in writing, an effort shall be made by both parties to settle this dispute. If no settlement is reached at the end of such forty-five (45) day period, or at the end of any mutually extended period, the Union shall have the right to call a general strike during a period of forty-five (45) days thereafter, but if such right to strike is not exercised before the end of the forty-five day period, the right to strike shall cease to exist and the grievance shall be determined settled on the basis of the Company's last answer or latest proposal.

Borg-Warner Corporation, Mechanics Universal Joint Division/United Auto Workers

The experience of the involved parties with this particular clause is not at hand. However, given the nature of some labor-management relationships, a company might use such a clause to set a record for repeated 45-day feats of breath-holding.

NO-STRIKE LITIGATION

The Supreme Court has lavishly upheld the contractual integrity of the no-strike pledge in a few landmark cases, the most important of which is *Local 174, Teamsters Union* v. *Lucas Flour Company* (1962).[37] In that case, a collective agreement between the union and company provided for arbitration over "any difference as to the true interpretation of this agreement" and stated that, "during such arbitration, there shall be no suspension of work." Another paragraph of the arbitration article provided that, "should any difference arise between the employer and the employee, same shall be submitted to arbitration . . . ," but nothing was said about work stoppages.

When the company fired an employee under an article in the agreement that reserved to management "the right to discharge" for unsatisfactory work, the union struck in protest, but without success. Subsequently, the propriety of the discharge was arbitrated, and the arbiter's decision upheld the company's discharge action. In effect, both parties had agreed that the dispute was within the ambit of the arbitration article, since neither contested before the chosen arbitrator that the matter was nonarbitrable.

Later, the company sued the union in a state court for damages resulting from the strike. (This is the suit that certiorari brought to the U.S. Supreme Court.) The state tribunal applied local contract law and held that the union had broken its contract by striking when it did. The company also brought suit against the union in the Superior Court of King County, Washington, asking damages for business losses caused by the strike. After a trial, that court entered a judgment of $6,501.60 in favor of the employer.

On appeal, the judgment was affirmed by Department One of the Supreme Court of Washington,[38] which held that the pre-emption doctrine of *San Diego Building Trades Council* v. *Garman* [39] did not deprive it of jurisdiction over the controversy. The court further held that Section 301 of the Labor Management Relations Act could not reasonably be interpreted as pre-empting state jurisdiction, or as affecting it by limiting the substantive law to be applied.[40] (Section 301 has been interpreted to provide that "Suits for violation of contracts between an employer and a labor organization representing employees in an industry affecting commerce . . . may be brought in any district court of the United States having jurisdiction of the parties, without respect to the amount in controversy or without regard to the citizenship of the parties.") [41] Expressly applying principles of state law, the court reasoned that the strike was a violation of the collective bargaining contract, because it was an attempt to coerce the employer to forgo his contractual right to discharge an employee for unsatisfactory work.

However, when the *Lucas Flour* case came before the U.S. Supreme Court, it reasoned that the state courts' choice of law was clearly improper. Its *Lincoln Mills* case [42] had held that the primary rights and duties of the parties to a collective agreement were regulated by federal law where suit was brought in a federal court under Section 301. In other words, primary rights and duties could not be governed by different laws merely because of the accident of the choice of a forum.

The strike was in breach of the contract, the Court ruled, because the agreement "expressly imposed upon both parties the duty of submitting the dispute in question to final and binding arbitration." Therefore, a no-strike promise was implied.

The Court advanced two reasons in support of this rule of law. One was freedom of contract: "To hold otherwise would obviously do violence to accepted principles of traditional contract law." This assertion was without any citation.

The other reason was industrial peace: "Even more in point," said the Court, "a contrary view would be completely at odds with the basic policy of national legislation to promote the arbitral process as a substitute for economic warfare." This assertion was supported by a citation to the case of *United Steelworkers Union* v. *Warrior & Gulf*

Navigation Company, a landmark Supreme Court case on the breadth and scope of arbitration clauses in labor-management contracts.[43] In effect, the Court's *Lucas Flour* rule prohibited by fiat strikes over arbitrable grievances.

One might assume that the Supreme Court's generous construction of the arbitration and no-strike promises would further the quest for industrial peace by deterring breach of contract. But the record does not bear this out. In this regard, one spokesman's remarks seem to be particularly relevant:

Quite apart from the important policy questions that a prohibition against strikes raises for a free society . . . , another consideration must be taken into account: it is impossible to carry out such a policy in America. . . . Union members can always find other ways than the formal, legal strike for achieving their purposes even over the opposition of their leaders. If they are sufficiently ingenious, they can always slow down operations legally, and if this is done by enough employees it will have the same effect as an actual strike. . . .[44]

Evidently, when workers' feelings run high, their actions will not be governed by such legal restraints as contractual no-strike promises. Despite the presence of these clauses—whether conditional or unconditional—the acts they seek to prevent are commonplace on the American industrial scene. The implications of such illegal acts, which are indeed far-reaching, are examined in the next chapter.

5
VIOLATIONS of the NO-STRIKE PLEDGE

DESPITE THE FACT that the wildcat strike (the strike in violation of the contract) is a serious offense, many such strikes are reported in the United States each year. In addition, unreported wildcat strikes must number in the hundreds, if not thousands, annually. We have developed in the United States the machinery for peaceful settlement of disputes over grievances and during contract negotiations. But in many instances we insist on resorting to that "shootout at the corral" mentality characteristic of Frontier days (at least in grade B Westerns), in which economic force is viewed as the most effective means of resolving labor-management problems.

No company can afford to condone strikes which violate the no-strike commitment, and management's right to penalize employees for participating in them is clearly established. The contractual responsibilities of the union with regard to illegal work stoppages are also clear. Of course, the union may be unable or unwilling to comply with the requirements of the contract, and the employer would then be compelled to seek other avenues of remedy, such as discharge, discipline, damage suits, the injunction, and arbitration.

The early sections of this chapter will deal with the responsibilities of the union and remedies for the employer when wildcat strikes occur. Later in the chapter *a number of practical measures which an employer can take to cope with a strike are listed,* as are the duties of law enforcement officers in such situations.

THE UNION'S RESPONSIBILITIES

This brief extract from a labor agreement briefly but forcefully states the union's obligation to seek to end a wildcat strike or other illegal "interruption of work":

In any case where an interruption of work occurs in violation of this Contract, the Union agrees that it will in good faith and without delay exert itself to bring about a quick termination of such interruptions of work, and will insist that the employee or employees involved therein return to work and resume normal operations promptly. To that end, the Local and International will promptly take whatever affirmative action is necessary.

International Harvester Company/United Auto Workers

The method by which the union is to disavow violations of the no-strike pledge is highlighted in this next example:

Upon receipt of notice from the Company, the Union hereby agrees that it will immediately disavow, through its officers and/or representatives any violation of Section 1 (no-strike clause) and will take positive measures to prevent and/or terminate any such violation by an employee or group of employees through, but without being limited thereto, the posting of notices, newspaper and radio announcements and other communications to the employee that the Union does not support such violations.

ITT Abrasive Products Company/United Steelworkers of America (expired June, 1975)

Obviously, the fact that such measures are required by a contract does not guarantee that a union will effectively carry them out—or even carry them out at all. But of course, the union is not the employer's last recourse when wildcat strikes actually occur.

THE DAMAGE SUIT

Historically, because of the former ready availability of the labor injunction remedy, the number of damage suits based on strike or boycott actions has not been large. For a number of reasons, employers generally preferred the injunction to the damage suit. An injunction could prevent a strike at its inception; it was not necessary to wait until damages had been sustained. Moreover, if a union violated an injunction, contempt proceedings could be instituted leading to fines against the union or even imprisonment of union officers or members. However, the federal

Norris—La Guardia Act and similar state laws have of course limited the use of the injunction only to those labor disputes where public order is threatened or certain Labor Management Relations Act violations occur.

Another deterrent to extensive use of damage suits against unions was the common law rule that unions, like other unincorporated associations, could not be sued in their common name. Instead, relief had to be sought against the individual members. This rule no longer applies in the federal courts and in many state courts.

Since the Taft-Hartley Act was adopted in 1947, federal courts have had express jurisdiction of suits for violation of collective bargaining agreements. In damage suits under Section 301 of the LMRA the courts have jurisdiction even though the breach of contract may also constitute an unfair labor practice. (For the text of Section 301, see Appendix 3.) Although Section 301 provides that damage suits may be brought against employers as well as unions, most suits to date have been brought against unions.

Unions have been very fearful of the possibility of such suits, and understandably so, especially since under the Taft Act a union can be held liable even for unauthorized strikes in violation of the contract. The following contract extracts will help to illustrate how some labor-management parties have dealt with conditions under which the union would not be liable:

The Union agrees that the waiver of the right of the Company to collect damages in the event of a "wildcat" strike is made only on condition that the Union, its officers, shop stewards, and other agents as specified in the foregoing shall promptly take such reasonable action as may be requested by the Company to prevent the occurrence of or to stop the continuance of an actual or imminent "wildcat" strike. However, a steward who participates in such a strike will be immediately removed from that office by the Union, will be subject to discharge without recourse, and the Union will be held blameless for his act. Such reasonable action shall include the following: (a) Requesting thru personal contact or meeting with employees that they comply with the contract and do not take part in a "wildcat" strike; (b) Notification to all employees in the event of a strike, that the strike is unauthorized and in violation of the Contract; (c) Public announcement in the local newspapers and on the local radio that the strike is unauthorized and not condoned by the Union; (d) Requesting the strikers to return to work and comply with the Contract.

Auburn Plastics/International Association of Machinists (expired May, 1975)

The final two examples are interesting for their significant contrast. The first, which reflects a charitable mutual attitude, provides for a flat waiver of recourse to court action:

In consideration of this Agreement, the IBEW agrees not to sue the Company, its officers, or representatives, and the Company agrees not to sue the IBEW, its officers, agents, or members for any labor matters in any court of law or equity.

Radio Corporation of America/International Brotherhood of Electrical Workers

The union in the next example apparently did not feel so benevolent on this subject when it bargained for the following contract provision:

The Union may (in addition to pursuing other remedies) sue the Employer in the Union's own behalf or in behalf of any aggrieved employee for specific performance of this Agreement, injunctive relief, recovery of dues, wages, vacations, or other benefits or any other legal redress, and the employee hereby expressly waives the right to object to the Union being party plaintiff in such action.

Cartage Exchange of Chicago, Illinois/Chicago Truck Drivers

THE INJUNCTION AND OTHER REMEDIES

The unions' awesome regard for Section 301 of the LMRA may not be limited to its damage suit provisions. It has been established that under Section 301 the federal district courts also have power to compel specific performance of the arbitration or any other provisions of a collective bargaining agreement. Thus, in conjunction with that authority, the courts may temporarily enjoin a strike over either a grievance (or what should be a grievance) or an existing-contract dispute when there is automatic recourse to arbitration provided in the contract. This may be done despite the Norris–La Guardia Act, which, the federal courts hold, deprives them of jurisdiction to enjoin the breach of a no-strike clause as such.

The federal courts will also uphold an arbitration award which enjoins slowdowns by a union subject to a no-strike clause. In so doing, the courts point out that there is no reason why either unions or employers should deny injunctive powers to the special arbitration tribunals which both parties have voluntarily created.

The employer has recourse to other remedies in addition to his ability to recover for provable damages from breach of contract and to insure specific performance of arbitration clauses. He may also bring charges before state courts (under their police power) and federal courts (on his own petition or that of the National Labor Relations Board) for the following acts committed by strikers: torts against the employer's property and violence and mass picketing. When Sections 7,2(13), 8(b)(1), 8(b)(2), and 10(j) of the LMRA are considered together, they mean that:

1. A union may be charged with responsibility for any act by its members or officers in any area of labor relations or on the picket line—even if the act was not authorized or approved by the union, and without the need for provability under historic tests of agency.

2. Every employee has a right to refrain from participating in strikes or other union activities, and it is an unfair labor practice for a union to coerce him to so participate.

3. Unfair labor practices such as mass picketing or any form of actual or threatened violence or coercion are prohibited. Any employer, or anyone claiming to be threatened or intimidated by a union or its members, may file a complaint of an

unfair labor practice with the NLRB. When the complaint is issued and there is reasonable cause to believe a violation of Taft-Hartley has occurred, the NLRB is empowered to petition any federal district court for appropriate temporary relief —regardless of the ability of the local police to cope with the problem, and the court may grant the injunction requested by the NLRB despite the Norris-La Guardia Act. [Sections 8(b), (c), and (d)—Unfair Labor Practices—appear as Appendix 4.]

In the following sections several relevant cases will be reviewed which serve to demonstrate how management has reacted to wildcat strikes and how arbitrators, the NLRB, and the courts have ruled with regard to those actions taken by management.

RULINGS BY ARBITRATORS

Labor problems, like taxes, are inevitable and inescapable. Since labor problems are invariably the results of a complex of economic, sociological, and historical forces and influences, there is no pattern to which they conform, nor is there a talismanic guide to solutions which guarantees a stable and secure pattern of labor-management relationships. The labor-relations process is a dynamic one which permits neither the problems nor the remedies to remain static.

Has the arbitration process been able to adapt to that dynamic process? The following statement by Harold W. Davey, professor of economics and director of the Industrial Relations Center at Iowa State University, provides a plausible answer:

> With due respect to the courts, damage suits, injunctive solutions and other specialized institutions cannot serve the cause of constructive collective bargaining as well as arbitration unless we who believe in the process undermine it by failing to correct certain shortcomings. . . .
>
> One critical question is whether arbitration, a process that is predicated on the *single standard* inherent in the labor relations jurisprudence concept, can survive and flourish in an era that provides multiple alternatives and which has encouraged some to argue that the process has become too institutionalized and establishment-oriented to cope effectively and fairly with such explosive issues as those involving charges of racial or sex discrimination.
>
> I submit that the evidence suggests arbitration *can* adapt to changing customs, life styles, work values and the like. *The more pertinent question is whether the negotiators and administrators of agreements can adapt.* It is at the bargaining table where the innovation and imagination equal to contemporary needs must be demonstrated. . . .[45]

Some of the evidence that arbitration does work is provided by the cases described in the following subsections.

Discharge and Discipline

As has been observed, there is little question regarding a company's right to discipline and discharge workers for violating a no-strike pledge in the labor agreement.* Where arbitrators have been asked to rule on the propriety of disciplinary action against such employees, they have sustained the company's action in the overwhelming majority of cases.

Customarily the issue before the arbitrator in such disputes is whether the employer was arbitrary or discriminatory in his selection of those to be disciplined or discharged. Arbiters have usually ruled that a company cannot single out a striker for discipline or heavier punishment *unless* it can be proved that he demonstrated leadership of the strike.[46] In one case where certain workers were discharged for striking while others were penalized less stringently, the action of the company was sustained by the arbitrator. He pointed out that the degree of punishment meted out to the workers was proportional to the extent of their leadership and responsibility for misconduct during the strike.[47]

In one typical case the employer discharged 24 employees who had walked out during their shift and then picketed the plant for five weeks. The union contended that there were many unsettled grievances concerning health, safety, and discrimination. The arbitrator upheld the discharges be-

---

* The company may replace with impunity employees who engage in an economic strike. In contrast, if the company dismisses those who participate in an unfair-labor-practice strike, they must be reinstated. In fact, jobs must be made for them if need be, even if hired replacements have to be dismissed.

cause the grievants were the instigators of a strike affecting the entire plant and had violated the no-strike clause and disrupted the grievance procedure.[48]

It is now fairly widely accepted that when an employee is asked by management to do something he believes is contrary to the collective bargaining agreement, he should nevertheless obey instructions and then file a grievance. (There are of course recognized exceptions to this rule: any action that jeopardizes the employee's—or his fellow workers'—health, safety, or welfare or that is indecent, illegal, immoral, and the like. Also, a contract itself may provide that an employee may short-circuit the usual formalities of the grievance procedure in some particularly critical situation which the parties have agreed should be dealt with virtually on the spot.) [49] It is particularly difficult to justify an employee's disobedience when the parties have taken the trouble to set up a grievance procedure and arbitration machinery to correct management's mistakes.

Here is a case in point: Some employees refused an order to work temporarily in another department because they believed the order violated the collective bargaining agreement, and the employer imposed a disciplinary layoff for breach of the no-strike pledge. The arbiter sustained the layoff and emphasized that despite their belief, the employees were not entitled to refuse to work but should have invoked the established grievance procedure.[50]

Responsibilities of Union Officials

Arbitrators generally recognize that local union officials have responsibilities beyond those of other employees. They are not only expected to perform their regular jobs but also to enforce the contract and influence other employees to comply with its terms. And when a union official participates in an unauthorized work stoppage, his offense is considered graver than that of the other employees.[51] In a situation where the employer suspended a shop steward for engaging in a strike in violation of the agreement, Arbitrator Arthur Hiller said:

The proposition that affirmative obligations of leadership in upholding the grievance procedure and opposing work stoppages devolved upon an employee, who by reason of seniority and status as a union officer must be held to have achieved a position of influence, has hitherto found acceptance under this and other agreements. Implicit in it is the thought that if those prominent and influential in the affairs of the union fail to so support these vital provisions of the agreement, the parties' expectations that they will be complied with during the life of the agreement become altogether illusory.[52]

Some arbitrators have viewed as a punishable offense not only a union official's active participation in an illegal strike but also his passive behavior ("negative leadership") in the face of known employee violations of the contract. For example, in a case in which the local union president, union committeeman, and shop steward were disciplined for failing to prevent an unauthorized work stoppage, Arbitrator Pearce Davis said:

. . . local union officials are the spokesmen for the workers. They are their leaders. They, therefore, have responsibilities over and beyond those of the rank and file. Local union officials are obligated aggressively to oppose actions that violate commitments undertaken in good faith. Local union officials are bound by virtue of their office to set personal examples of opposition to contract violation. They cannot be passive; they must vigorously seek to prevent contract violations by their constituents.[53]

In other words, a union representative has a special obligation to observe and respect the agreement. It is his contractually recognized function to protect employees in the grievance procedure against violations of that agreement by management. The agreement gives him special rights and privileges in order that he may perform that function. He cannot with impunity turn his back on the very agreement it is his duty to defend.

By virtue of his office, a union representative is a leader; indeed, it is reasonable to assume that it is because he is a leader that he acquires his union office. It follows inescapably that when he participates in a work stoppage—or makes no effort to prevent or end it—he is setting an example for the other employees. By his action—or inaction—he is indicating that the stoppage has his approval. This is a graver offense than participation by an ordinary employee and justifies a more serious penalty.[54]

Denial of Contract Benefits

Does participation in a wildcat strike justify the company's denying strikers all the protective provisions of the contract—that is, by such participation have the workers terminated their service under the contract and ceased to be employees? To date this issue remains unresolved, with arbitrators ruling both ways.[55]

Some employers who withhold contract benefits after an illegal work stoppage do so on the following premise: The employees have violated their guarantee not to strike during the term of the agreement, and therefore the company is excused from keeping its promises to provide the benefits in question.

That position may be an outgrowth of a rule of contract law which holds that when party A is responsible for committing a substantial breach of an agreement, it cannot bring an action against party B for B's subsequent failure to perform under that contract. However, this holds true only when the breach involves a promise or condition whose performance depended on the mutual performance of its promises by party B. In other words, that rule is not generally applicable to the enforcement of a labor agreement, as the following case illustrates:

When some employees engaged in a work stoppage halfway through the day after a holiday, the employer denied them holiday pay, claiming they had not met the contract conditions for paid holidays. The contract provided that, in order to receive holiday pay, employees had to work on the day preceding and the day following the holiday. The employees were not qualified to be paid for that holiday, the employer argued, because they had worked only half of the succeeding day.

However, the arbitrator rejected this argument on the grounds that (1) the contract did not state that employees had to work the full day to qualify for holiday pay, and (2) the usual purpose of requiring work on days surrounding a holiday is to discourage employees from stretching a holiday, but the work stoppage was not related to any desire to stretch the holiday. He further ruled that the employer's right to discipline employees for a work stoppage in violation of the contract did not include the right to deny them holiday pay for which they had qualified under the contract. Therefore, he ruled, in the absence of express contract language to the contrary, the denial of holiday pay was not included in the term "discipline" as contemplated by the agreement.[56]

Under most agreements, as was true in the case just cited, the parties did not intend that employee benefits be dependent on the employees' keeping their pledge under the no-strike article. To make such an intention effective, the company would probably have to point to contract language which expressly states that violations of the no-strike clause will result in the denial of contractual benefits. In the absence of such a provision, an arbitrator could not justifiably uphold their denial. To do so would be to imply that, although the contract continued to be in effect, the employees' prior contract breach relieved the company of its contractual responsibility in the event of future contract violations by the employees.

Injunctions and Damages

In appropriate circumstances, the power to enjoin an illegal work stoppage or to award damages to the employer for his losses is held by both the federal courts and the arbitrator. In the following statement, Professor Davey compares such court- and arbitrator-imposed remedies:

. . . the utility of damage suits under Sections 301 and 303 [of the LMRA] has always been a questionable avenue for remedial relief. It is seldom used except in situations that have already degenerated, perhaps beyond repair. As to the speed of damage suits, arbitral relief is quicker and less bruising to the relationship. Arbitrators can be given authority to assess damages. They can do so more expeditiously than can the courts, even under current conditions where delay is a major source of dissatisfaction with arbitration as a process.

Injunctive relief against "wildcats" under Boys Markets [U.S. Supreme Court decision] reasoning will doubtless be of value to *some* employers in getting true value from their contracts. Here again, however, I see no reason why union contracts should not be negotiated to provide for instant arbitration in "wildcat" cases. The arbitrator can be empowered by contract to assess blame, discipline and damages for proven failure to comply with a no-strike clause.

In summary, the "other" legal remedies do not stand up on balance to a properly devised system of grievance arbitration. . . .[57]

A review of the few published holdings and the decisions they reflect appears to lend substance and credence to Professor Davey's claim. Here are some relevant cases in which arbitrators issued injunctions or imposed damages against contract violators:

1. When members of a local union struck the General American Transportation Corp. and members of a sister local refused to cross the picket lines, Arbitrator Harry Abrahams enjoined those acts, ruling that they constituted a strike and work stoppage in violation of the contract's no-strike article.[58]

2. When local-union members at a Ford Motor Company plant struck in violation of the contract's no-strike clause, Arbitrator Harry Platt ordered the local, its officers, and its members to cease and desist from participating in the strike, from picketing, and from inducing other employees to engage in the strike.[59]

3. To a newspaper publisher whose employees had engaged in a wildcat strike, Arbitrator Monroe Berkowitz awarded $5,000 in damages, including the amount of a previous fine against the union. Suspended after a similar incident, that fine became payable on the recurrence of a work stoppage. However, the arbitrator's total award was less than the publisher's direct damages because the union officials had made genuine efforts to persuade the employees to return to work.[60]

4. For damages directly caused by the union's strike in breach of its contract, Arbitrator Paul Kleinsorge awarded an employer the amount

which the employer accounted for at the arbitration hearing. However, the arbitrator ruled that the employer was not entitled to an award of damages for loss of goodwill, since the computation of those damages was based on an estimate and was not supported by adequate proof of loss.[61]

RULINGS BY THE NLRB

In a recent case a union engaged in a work stoppage and threatened another in order to force the employer to appoint a certain employee as foreman either in place of the general foreman or under him. The National Labor Relations Board held that the union's conduct was in violation of the Taft-Hartley Act because it was meant to restrain or coerce the employer in the selection of his representative in collective bargaining or the adjustment of grievances.

In so ruling, the Board rejected a contention that the union's conduct should not be deemed unlawful because it "was in response to intolerable racial discriminatory working conditions imposed upon the employees by the general foreman." The Board observed: "At all times the employees were free under Sections 7 and 13 of the Act to invoke their statutory rights" to engage in a strike or any other concerted activity to protest the general foreman's alleged discriminatory practices. However, it added, these rights did not include "the right to dictate to an employer the selection of a particular supervisor . . . who would have the power to engage in collective bargaining or adjust grievances." [62]

It should be pointed out that the Board was referring only to the union's *statutory right* under the Act to strike in protest against alleged discriminatory practices. Without a careful look at the labor agreement in question, it cannot be stated that the union also had a *contractual right* to strike over this issue.

In a number of early cases the NLRB, with the approval of the courts, established the principle that a concerted refusal to perform overtime work is a partial strike unprotected by the Taft-Hartley Act. Describing this tactic as an attempt by the employees to work on terms prescribed solely by themselves, the Board held that their discharge was not a violation of the Act.[63]

RULINGS BY THE COURTS

Under ideal conditions, labor disputes would always be settled by the parties themselves, through their grievance machinery, or with the help of a third party, the arbitrator. However, when the grievance-arbitration process is unable to resolve a dispute, for whatever reason, it invariably becomes a matter for the courts.

Refusal of Overtime

Like the NLRB, the courts have also dealt with the refusal by employees to work overtime. One such case involved a union and an employer association whose agreement provided that overtime should not be worked except when unavoidable. When union members refused to work overtime on the ground that it was avoidable, the dispute was submitted to an arbiter, who ruled that it should be resolved in the courts.

The federal district court which decided the case noted that the union's members performed overtime services when requested for 29 months prior to their refusal without once questioning their avoidability. This conduct, the court said, seemed to be clear and unmistakable evidence that the parties intended to construe their contract as requiring some overtime as part of the normal work relationship. The refusal to work overtime thus constituted a strike, the court decided, and it enjoined that tactic as a violation of the contract's no-strike clause. Rejecting a 1939 court decision to the contrary, the court observed:

In today's complicated interplay between management and labor to say that merely because men are working they are not striking is too easy. It does not take into account that performing less work than they have under a contract in existence for years and upon which management has relied is a refined form of torture every bit as destructive as a strike. It is a strike.[64]

Unions' Duty to End Strikes

In this case a federal district court ruled that an international union and a local union that had a no-strike clause in their collective bargaining contract had a duty to use "every reasonable means" to end a wildcat strike even though the contract did not explicitly set forth such a duty. The court further found that these unions breached their duty by failing to take sufficient steps to end unauthorized strikes by their members.

Taking note of the no-strike clause, the court said it is reasonable to infer that a representative of employees has an obligation to take whatever reasonable measures are available and indicated to prevent or bring to an end activity engaged in by its members in which it as an entity is not free to engage.

Despite the fact that both the local and the international urged the wildcat strikers to return to work, the court said, they failed to use many other and potentially more effective approaches. Among other things, it pointed out that the local could have removed the stewards and committeemen who were organizing and leading the strike, insured that no strikers were elsewhere employed during the strike, imposed daily fines on all strikers, and taken votes by secret ballot on whether to end the strike. The international could have threatened to discipline, and imposed discipline on, the strikers. It could also have acted sooner in sending representatives to urge the dissidents to let other workers return to work and in calling a meeting in its national office, the court said.[65]

Reversal of an Injunction

This dispute between a union and contractors involved applicable wage rates for certain work and was originally submitted by the union to the contract grievance procedure. However, the labor agreement did not provide for mandatory arbitration of disputes that were not resolved by the grievance procedure, and when the procedure deadlocked, the union went on strike.

The contractors reacted by obtaining an injunction from a federal district court, which based its action on the Supreme Court's *Boys Markets* decision.[66] *Boys Markets* authorizes the courts to enjoin certain strikes despite the Norris-La Guardia Act.

However, when the case came before the U.S. Court of Appeals in Chicago, it determined that the district court had improperly enjoined the strike. The *Boys Markets* decision, the court of appeals pointed out, is limited to situations where a contract contains a mandatory grievance-adjustment or arbitration procedure. The contract in question contained no such provision—in fact, the union expressly reserved the right to "economic recourse" in the event of a deadlock—and therefore *Boys Markets* was inapplicable.[67] The court concluded that the controversy was a labor dispute within the meaning of the Norris-La Guardia Act not only when it arose but also after the union's exhaustion of the grievance procedure.

A Strike without Legitimate Purpose

In this last, but not least, of the court cases reviewed in this section, a strike was declared in breach of contract despite the fact that the contract contained neither a no-strike clause nor a settlement-of-disputes provision.

The union began the strike in order to force the employer to comply with contractual provisions concerning payments to the union trust funds. A few months later, the employer tendered payment, but the strike continued for approximately two years because the union also demanded payment of the wages of a driver who was idled by the strike. In the end, the employer was forced to cease all operations, to sell its equipment, and to suffer revocation of its Interstate Commerce Commission certificate of public convenience and necessity.

Addressing the union's initial purpose in striking, a federal district court declared:

Stripped of all but the essentials, a collective bargaining agreement represents a purchase by an employer of labor for his business, and the basic promise made by a union in every such agreement is that it will provide the employer with men to work. Any action by the union in derogation of this promise can only be justified by a breach by the employer of a significant obligation on his part.

Such a breach by the employer had in fact occurred in the instant case, the court conceded. It found, however, that the union in turn had violated the contract by insisting unjustifiably on the payment of moneys (the driver's wages) not due as a condition for settling the strike and thereby continuing the strike beyond the date on which the employer tendered payment for the trust funds. The court explained:

There is no place in the national labor policy for strikes which serve no legitimate labor purpose. Yet that is the kind of strike that was waged by the union once the employer admitted its delinquency and offered to pay all that it owed under the terms of its contract. At that point continuance of the strike could not be justified. The initial violation by the employer and the claim as to the employee's wages became a pretext for the purpose

121

of punishing the employer; for the purpose of exacting from it a substantially larger sum of money than it rightly owed; for the purpose of demonstrating the power of this union over those with whom it did business.[68]

In conclusion, in the court's view the fact that the contract was silent on the means of settling disputes did not entitle the union to strike over unimportant matters.

PRACTICAL MEASURES FOR THE EMPLOYER

A wildcat strike is an emergency situation which creates special and often unprecedented problems. Ofttimes it catches management by surprise. However, it is nevertheless advisable to be properly organized for such an emergency to avoid confusion, duplication of effort, and a breakdown in communications. The following checklist is designed to aid the employer to cope with a wildcat strike by fortifying him with the essential "do's" and "don'ts":

1. During the period of the work stoppage it is usually unwise to engage in discussions with the union about the merits of the matter that allegedly precipitated the illegal action. By taking the law into their own hands, the employees and the union have raised an issue—the illegal breach of the no-strike clause—that must precede any consideration of the merits of the dispute.

If discussion is permitted on the merits of the problem, management is enabling the union to hold a gun to its head, a weapon presumably removed from the union's arsenal. Once the union and employees have determined that they can accomplish their objectives by the unlawful use of this economic force and can obtain concessions or additional contractual or extracontractual benefits, there will be no end to their utilization of this tactic.

Under normal circumstances, the refusal of the employer to discuss with the appropriate union officials an actual or a potential grievance can be construed as a refusal to bargain in good faith. But the circumstances surrounding this type of dispute are anything but normal and, in fact, constitute an emergency situation. The union should be made to understand that the contractual grievance processes will be instantly implemented, and in good faith, only after a complete return to work.

2. Obviously, the provisions of the collective bargaining agreement must be reviewed regarding work stoppages and a determination made of the extent of the contract violations.

3. Customarily the local union officers and then the international union representatives, if any, are notified of the existence of a work stoppage in violation of the labor agreement. At the same time, union assistance is demanded in bringing about the immediate resumption of plant operations.

4. Presumably, management will be taking steps toward obtaining injunctive relief, compensatory or punitive damages, and the like.[69] Local management representatives usually consult with the industrial relations department and with corpo-

rate legal advisors or other labor counsel concerning the company's legal position and possible legal action.

A complete record of strike damages should be maintained, as well as an estimate of the loss of production, a record of canceled orders, and the like.

Usually an attempt is made to determine the leaders and instigators of the illegal strike action and any persons who engage in violence, interference, or intimidation so that appropriate disciplinary action may be taken under the contract.

However, an employer should not blame *all* of his employees nor ever make plans to punish them the first chance he gets. They are the people the company depends on to run the shop. The odds are that many of the workers are as unhappy over the affair as the employer is. Trying to see things from their point of view may provide insights into the problem and initiate ideas for potential settlements.

Often a management communication is issued to all participating employees describing the illegal nature of the work stoppage and the company action already taken to end the stoppage, or to be taken if the stoppage continues beyond a given time.

Consideration is often given to calling in the Federal Mediation and Conciliation Service and/or the state mediation agency.

The foregoing recommendations deal with illegal strikes. However, there are matters for management to consider which are applicable to *legal* as well as illegal strikes. The list which follows is not intended to be all inclusive but makes mention of the more important considerations:

Employers who choose to involve the news media and the community in discussing the issues should use a press-liaison specialist to prepare press releases. Only one press-liaison officer should be chosen, and only he should be authorized to issue written or oral statements to the news media.

A word of caution must be offered here: It is wise to guard against releases which indicate that the company will not budge another inch or which indiscriminately convey ultimatums—unless the company is prepared to meet any resulting developments.

1. Some plan must be implemented for plant maintenance during the strike. Consideration must be given to such functions as heating and protection against fire and property damage. There may even be a need to establish facilities for supervisors "living in" during the strike.

2. It may be desirable, or even necessary to keep vendors, customers, sales force, transportation officials, and sometimes even stockholders informed on the issues and implications of the strike. Some employers have even sought the aid of competitors to supply their customers' needs for the duration of the strike.

3. Sometimes there must be a plan for the handling of benefits to employees, such as group insurance benefits and pensions.

4. It often becomes necessary to develop a plan

for handling incoming and outgoing mail, material, and inventory. If regular common carriers renege on commitments, can others be found or should a protest be made to the ICC?

5. Management may have to ask itself if there is a likelihood that the strikers will persuade employees in other company divisions or operations to strike in sympathy.

6. If the employer does not have a policy, it may have to make a decision about nonunion personnel, supervisors, and unionized employees who report to work. Can they continue to work? If so, where and for how long? If they cannot work, will they be paid? How will preparation of payrolls be handled? Will there be any special personnel-transportation problems, and what accommodations, if any, can be made?

It is important also for management to consider the attitudes and fears of its nonstriking employees. They need to be told what lies ahead for them in terms of job security. They want to know. If they can be reassured, it will certainly boost their morale. Even if it becomes necessary to lay some of them off, it should be in accord with some well-conceived and fairly executed plan, and not on a hit-or-miss basis.

A decision will be needed on the time, method, and place of payment to striking employees of their last-earned wages.

If access to the plant becomes too difficult, management may have to devise a plan for locating management headquarters, a command post, and communication and printing facilities away from the plant site.

Many employers plan on having observers, cameras, stenographers, and tape recorders available to record instances of violent or mass picketing. Such records can be used as evidence in injunction proceedings and to substantiate charges for which disciplinary action is taken.

It is advisable to keep the plant switchboard and teletype equipment open if possible. The personnel manning such equipment should be given clear instructions on how to handle various incoming calls and inquiries.

The mayor, chief of police, sheriff, state police, or other law officials should be contacted to determine what kind of help is available for the protection of nonunion personnel and supervisors who may choose to, or be required to, work during the strike. If plant guards are also union organized, does their labor agreement require them to work? Is there a provision in their contract which postpones its expiration if other employees are on strike? If plant guards are supplied by a detective firm, can it cancel its contract during a strike at the plant?

The company's relations with law enforcement officials during strikes are often important and frequently include public relations aspects. Of course, it is important for the company to know just what are the responsibilities of the police at such times. The following section deals with that topic.

DUTIES OF LAW ENFORCEMENT OFFICERS

It is the responsibility of the police—whether a local police or sheriff's department or the state police—to see that certain basic rules of behavior are observed by those conducting or participating in labor controversies, strikes, or picket lines:

1. People working in or having business with plants which are on strike have a right to pass freely in and out of the plant.

2. Pickets should not in any way block a door, passageway, driveway, crosswalk or other entrance or exit to a struck plant or place of business.

3. Union officials or pickets have a right to talk to people going in or out of a struck plant. However, intimidation, threats, and coercion are not permitted, and no one is required to do what the strikers demand.

4. Fighting, assault, battery, violence, threat, or intimidation is not permissible under the law.

5. Carrying firearms, knives, clubs, and other dangerous weapons is not permissible under the law.

6. Sound trucks should not be permitted to be unduly noisy, should have a permit, and should keep moving.

7. Profanity on streets and sidewalks is a violation of the law.

8. Anyone who willfully blocks the sidewalks of or entrances to a plant is in violation of the law.

9. If acts of violence or trespass occur on company premises, plant officials may file complaints or seek an injunction. A victim of violence should sign a warrant for the arrest of the person or persons responsible.

10. Company officials should make every effort to permit individuals and vehicles to move in and out of the plant in a normal manner during a strike.

6
MISCONDUCT during STRIKES

THE MAJORITY of strikers are law-abiding citizens whose lawlessness does not go beyond an occasional parking ticket and the like. When such people go on strike, they are not instantly transformed into violent anarchists. Few, if any, among them will look for opportunities to engage in raw violence.

But a strike is a very emotional experience. The workers are without work and wonder how long they will continue to be without it. Often they see nonunion personnel and others doing their jobs while they are on the street. Because they realize this will extend the employer's ability to withstand the impact of the strike, they grow more anxious and insecure.

Most of the workers probably believe the union is right on the issues that generated the strike. But some may not agree and yet they feel obliged to, or fearful not to, go along with the leaders. The emotional turmoil, internal conflicts, and bitter frustrations that are typically present during a work stoppage combine to generate an atmosphere which brings out the worst in some and causes others to react in a manner inconsistent with their basic character.

This chapter will deal with strikers' misconduct in the eyes of the employer and with the reactions to such acts by the employer and by arbitrators and other neutrals. It will also deal with the misconduct of employees from the point of view of the union—that is to say, their strikebreaking activities and the union's reaction to such activities.

MISCONDUCT AMONG STRIKERS

Arbitrators are nearly unanimous in holding that employees who engage in misconduct during a strike, whether a legal or an illegal strike, are properly subject to discipline or discharge. Of course, the employer must come forward with sufficient evidence to establish the culpability of the disciplined employee. Often, but certainly not always, the offenses occur in connection with management's exercise of its legal right to continue to operate its enterprise during a strike. More often than not, they consist of the intimidation—by threats of violence—of workers who continue to perform their jobs during the strike. The performance of one's job during a strike is also a legal right.

In cases of misconduct it is the labor practitioner's responsibility to determine what penalty should be considered appropriate. According to Arbitrator J. Fred Holly,

A strike situation embraces an environment vastly different from that which exists in the daily relations of the parties. Generally, the workday principle that discharge is for just cause if it is not arbitrary, capricious or discriminatory has obvious shortcomings, when applied to employee's action during strikes. In the latter situation there is an absence of supervision; the atmosphere is emotionally charged, particularly if the employer exercises his right to keep his plant open; there is more ready availability of remedies at law; community attitudes and pressures bring an added force to bear on the parties. . . . As a consequence, acts of indiscretion and violence are to be more expected during strikes. Yet the expectation of incidents of violence does not remove the need for or the right to discipline. Violence is not to be condoned except under the most unusual circumstances. Given the aforementioned differences, however, disciplinary action short of discharge may be required in a strike situation, even though a similar act might warrant discharge in a normal work situation. Therefore, it is incumbent upon the arbitrator to examine all circumstances that exist in the strike situation before deciding upon the propriety of the discipline administered.[70]

Violence and Other Acts

In one dispute arising out of a wildcat strike, the Westinghouse Electric Corporation satisfied its arbiter that its discipline, which was "short of discharge," was appropriate. The strike began when employees failed to return to work after the lunch break. Pickets appeared at the plant gates about 2:00

131

P.M. An employee who normally reported to work about 2:45 had come in at 1:30 for an insurance refund and therefore had no knowledge that pickets were at the gates. He reported to his regular job, noting only that several of his fellow employees were absent. When he left the plant in his car at 11:45 that evening, a black sedan followed and pulled alongside. Its occupants then threw several rocks or heavy objects at his car, breaking the glass in two windows. There was sufficient light from street lamps for him to identify the people in the sedan.

After he reported the incident to a supervisor, one of the offending employees was given a ten-day disciplinary suspension and two others were each given a five-day suspension. Arbitrator Al T. Singletary upheld the company's action.[71]

In another case a striker allegedly trailed a car in which two supervisors were riding from a struck plant and attempted to force it off the road or into a truck ahead. The employee was discharged, but as the facts unfolded at the hearing, he had a plausible reason for following the supervisor's car from the plant. Evidence indicated the whole affair was the result of a "mutual misunderstanding," the employee believing that the supervisors in the car ahead and the car behind his own were trying to box him in, and the supervisors mistaking his moves to extricate his car as offensive tactics. As a result, the employee was reinstated with back pay.[72]

At the Southern Bell Telephone & Telegraph Company a striker entered the plant when employees were working, grabbed one and pointed a knife at him, saying he had been sent to "cut the employee's guts out." The company discharged him.

The arbiter ruled that even if the striker did intend only to "scare" the employee as claimed, his act constituted an immediate threat of great physical harm and was substantially beyond the limits of strike misconduct for which a penalty short of discharge was appropriate.[73]

At the same firm but a different arbitration forum, the discharge of a striker who assaulted a nonstriker was commuted to a one-week suspension because the evidence showed that the nonstriker provoked the assault by pushing the striker.[74] So here we have the mitigating circumstance of provocation, and the question of who really was the instigator and aggressor.

The misconduct of employees during an economic strike at a hospital took the form of sitdowns in the hospital administrator's office. This activity willfully violated a state court order prohibiting strikers from trespassing on hospital premises. Moreover, it was designed to force the hospital to recognize a union that had been unable to establish its majority status before the state court. The company discharged the sitdown participants, and at the hearing the arbiter held that they were guilty of serious misconduct and should be disciplined.[75] "Violence," he said, "is implicit in the very act of sitting down; no matter that there is no additional violence committed in its execution." The arbiter found the doctrine of the Supreme Court in another case to be of interest.

In that earlier case, a group of employees at Fansteel, Inc., was discharged after they had seized and held two key buildings. The Court supported their discharge, stating: "We are unable to conclude that Congress intended to compel employers to retain persons in their employ regardless of their unlawful conduct" or "to invest those who go on strike with an immunity from discharge for acts of trespass. . . ." [76]

Stealing, malicious destruction of company property, and similar offenses consistently have been held by arbitrators to be among actions justifying summary discharge rather than corrective discipline. Accordingly, a telephone company was held to have properly discharged two strikers who removed part of an outside coin telephone without authorization and carried it away. [77]

The opinion of an arbitrator in a General Electric Company case is perhaps unique, at least in the sense that it is the only one of its particular kind which the author's research of published cases uncovered.

In this dispute, the company imposed disciplinary suspensions on three union members for picket-line misconduct during an economic strike. The arbiter held that the employer's actions were not for just cause because in his opinion the company's right to exercise its disciplinary function was operative *only* during the time the employee was obligated to contribute to production. Since an economic strike was in progress, the workers were freed of this obligation. It was also significant to him that the company had kept its plant gates open and operated its business during the work stoppage. In this regard he commented:

Under the circumstances the Company's right to discipline employees engaged in an illegal strike where it itself is a contributor to a violence provoking environment can only be judged against the same criteria that are invoked by any citizen who takes measures to defend his property in a civil disturbance. The criteria of judgment expected are much more vigorous than in ordinary cases of alleged employee misbehavior under normal conditions.[78]

The arbiter concluded that the three disciplined employees should be reinstated with full back pay.

Holdings such as this are very infrequent, and this seems fortunate. It is regrettable that when a company exercises its *legal* right to operate its business, or an employee *his right* to pursue his livelihood, some perceive such a justifiable act as irresponsible and unreasonably provocative of the illegal conduct of others.

Crossing Picket Lines

As has already been covered, there is no doubt that a company may discipline and discharge employees who engage in illegal work stoppages and strikes. In this connection, if its labor agreement contains a no-strike clause,* it may punish workers

* Relatively few contracts devote special attention to the processing of work from or bound to struck or "unfair" plants, the crossing of picket lines by employees at their own or other plants, or the calling of sympathy strikes. In the main, such problems are handled indirectly in the contracts' general no-strike clause. Some contracts assert the right of employees to observe "legal" picket lines, or to observe picket lines where bodily harm might result from crossing them. Provisions sometimes state that the employer will not ask workers to violate either picket lines or boycotts. The Taft Act guarantees employees the right to refuse to cross a picket line at another plant if it is conducted in connection with an authorized strike of a certified union. (See "Basic Patterns in Union Contracts," Bureau of National Affairs Bulletin 590, January 11, 1968.)

who refuse to cross a picket line at another employer's place of business when such picketing is an unprotected activity under the Labor Management Relations Act.[79] Arbitration cases revolving on this particular issue reveal varying treatment.

When workers who refused to cross a picket line to perform installations at a customer's premises were suspended for two days by their employer, arbitrator Wayne Quinlan held that the company's action was not justified under the contract. The employees' refusal, he said, was not a "strike concerted plan for absence from work, or lockout," which the agreement banned. It was rather lawful activity which the company had agreed not to interfere with in its recognition clause. Moreover, the suspensions were not justified as a preservation of "efficient operation of its business," for no particular urgency attached to this job and the company had assigned no other workers to it but waited until the suspended employees had returned to work.[80]

Where the established picket line is that of another union, the right of employees to refuse to cross it may be determined by the language of their own agreement.

For example, in a dispute involving Sears, Roebuck and Co., the company was held by arbiter Arthur Miller to have violated the contract's no-strike promise when it would not reinstate employees who respected another union's picket lines. The contract in effect permitted workers to do this and provided for them to be placed on leaves of absence and to exercise their contractual seniority rights to regain jobs filled by replacements. Their action thus did not constitute grounds for discharge.[81]

Joseph T. Ryerson & Son, Inc., disciplined employees for participating in an "illegal strike" when they refused to cross another union's picket lines. Arbiter Edward A. Lynch ruled that the company did not have just cause. The disciplined employees had no control over the situation and did not instigate or participate in the picket line, and the company did not bring in uniformed policemen or provide other guarantees of their personal safety. Therefore, they had not violated the contract or mounted an illegal strike by refusing to cross the picket line.[82]

Arbitrator Henry W. Hoel saw the facts differently in another case, in which a worker was discharged for refusing to cross a peaceful picket line set up at a Hess Oil and Chemical Corporation plant:

The man was not a member of the picketing union. There was no solicitation of the company's employees by the pickets; the line was merely intended to inform the public that the employer was paying substandard wages to temporary workers. The grievant's union advised all members they could ignore the picket line because of their contract with the company, and all other employees crossed the line. In addition, the worker had already been warned that he would be discharged unless he reported to work.[83] Noting those facts, the arbiter upheld the discharge.

Conclusion

Although parties to labor agreements now enjoy a higher level of sophistication than at any time in the past 25 years, the number of cases like the ones illustrated here is alarmingly high. And of course, discipline and discharge continue to be the most frequently arbitrated issue. An analysis of such cases leads to the conclusion that each party still has a long way to go before it achieves sufficient understanding of its rights and responsibilities and those of the other party. Perhaps, in part, both have failed to assume their responsibility to develop their respective representatives, employees, and members and to educate them on their proper role and conduct. Perhaps all the parties—employer, employees, and union—have failed to realize that each is entitled to its respective positions and principles and philosophies, and that the only road to a peaceful and constructive relationship is that of mutual acceptance, respect, and understanding.

A word of caution to the employer: When striker misconduct occurs which is sufficient to merit discharge, such action should be taken with the realization that it may create an additional stumbling block to settling the strike. Invariably the union will defend these discharged workers. More often than not, they will demand their reinstatement as a condition for joining with management in a strike-settlement agreement. These words are not intended to dissuade an employer from taking that action which he believes is right, appropriate, and necessary. But one must be realistic about these matters and fully realize the continuing and perhaps long-range consequences of any contemplated action.

STRIKEBREAKING AND UNION-IMPOSED DISCIPLINE

The discipline a union imposes on its members may assume a variety of forms. It may consist of fines, it may involve a threat not to handle members' grievances, or it may be suspension or expulsion if the misconduct is extremely serious in the eyes of the union.

Management usually has no right to intervene either to support or oppose disciplinary action for violation of any union rules and bylaws except those concerning the payment of fees and dues under certain conditions.

As management may not intrude on the union's rights, so the labor organization may not encroach on the employer's preserves. But there is a troublesome gray area encompassing the job activities of a union member who is in a supervisory position, and this situation may provoke company-union disputes that are brought to arbitration.

The majority of the rare arbitration hearings on union discipline of members involve publishing firms and newspapers in contests with typographical unions. This may be explained in part by the fact that labor agreements between these parties commonly call for foremen to be union members as well. These employees often find themselves walking a thin line between their obligations as supervisors and semimembers of management and their loyalty to the labor organization. When the union's expectations of allegiance from them are not fulfilled, it will be likely to attempt to impose some disciplinary penalty.

With regard to a union threat not to handle grievances of members who fail to pay certain assessments, the NLRB has ruled that this amounts to unlawful restraint and coercion, for the processing of members' grievances is not an internal matter and therefore is not governed by the union's right to make its own rules. The Board has concluded that the union, as the exclusive representative of a bargaining unit, has the obligation to accept all grievances submitted to it by the employees it bargains for and to process them impartially and without discrimination.[84]

Pertinent Cases

During its 1972–1973 term, the U.S. Supreme Court took final action on 138 petitions presenting questions of labor law.[85] Three of the four Taft-Hartley cases in which the Court issued decisions in that term involved fines imposed by unions. The three rulings were as follows:

1. The NLRB was warranted in finding that a union unlawfully sought court enforcement of fines that it imposed on employees who engaged in strikebreaking activities after resigning from the union. Nothing in the record, the Court said, indicated that members were informed that a (union) constitutional provision applied by the union had been interpreted as imposing any obligation on

resigned members not to engage in strikebreaking for the duration of a union-called strike.[86]

2. The NLRB was warranted in finding that a union unlawfully fined employees who had re-signed from union membership during a lawful, au-thorized strike and then returned to work during the strike. Neither the union's collective bargain-ing contract with the employer nor its constitution and bylaws defined or limited the circumstances under which a member could resign from the union, the Court pointed out.[87]

3. The NLRB did not have the authority to de-termine whether a fine lawfully imposed by a union on a member is "reasonable" in amount; this was a matter for determination by the state courts. The Court said that Congress did not authorize the Board to "evaluate the fairness of union discipline meted out to protect a legitimate union interest" when that discipline did not interfere with the employer–employee relationship or otherwise vio-late a statutory policy. The Court stated:

Issues as to the reasonableness of such fines must be decided upon the basis of the law of contracts, voluntary associations, or such other principles of law as may be applied in a forum competent to adjudicate the issue. Under our holding, state courts will be wholly free to apply state law to such issues at the suit of either the union or the member fined.[88]

Section 8(b)(1)(A) of the Taft-Hartley Act makes it an unfair labor practice for a union to restrain or coerce employees in the exercise of rights guaran-teed in Section 7, including the right to refrain from engaging in concerted activities. There is a proviso, however, that Section 7 "shall not impair the right of a labor organization to prescribe its own rules with respect to the acquisition or retention of membership therein."

The most controversial case regarding the application of this proviso involved the Allis-Chalmers Manufacturing Company and the Auto Workers. The Supreme Court held that the union did not violate the Taft Act by imposing fines ranging from $20 to $100 on members who crossed a lawful picket line and by instituting legal proceedings against the members to collect the fines. Justice Brennan, who wrote the Court's opinion, reasoned that in many cases expulsion would be a far more coercive technique for enforcing a union rule and for collecting a reasonable fine than would be the threat of court enforcement.[89] (Expulsion is permitted by the proviso.)

Ever since the Supreme Court decided the *Allis-Chalmers* case, the courts and the NLRB have been developing nuances on the doctrine. For example, in late 1972 the U.S. Court of Appeals for the Sixth Circuit upheld an NLRB decision that a union engaged in unlawful restraint and coercion under Section 8(b)(1)(A) by requiring employees to pay one-third of their earnings to the union to obtain picket-line passes that would permit them to work during an economic strike called by the union. In so holding, the court of appeals made these points:

1. The union used unacceptable means to prevent the employees from working if they refused to make the one-third contribution.

2. No union member could escape the union's ostensibly internal rule by resigning from the union, since even nonmembers were subject to the union's coercion.

3. By its coercion, the union linked the employees' jobs with their organizational rights in that it prevented those not in sympathy with the union from working.

The court pointed out that in the *Allis-Chalmers* case the Supreme Court concluded that Section 8(b)(1)(A) was enacted primarily to control union conduct during organizational campaigns. More specifically, it was found to have been designed "to protect employees in their freedom to decide whether or not they desire to join labor organizations to prevent them from being restrained or coerced."

It may be assumed, the court continued, that a union may inaugurate a voluntary contribution program and request members and nonmembers to pay a portion of the wages they earn during a strike as a donation to the union's effort. But that was not the situation here. The union used unacceptable means to prevent employees without passes from working.[90]

Are supervisors who are union members performing a managerial function when they do rank-and-file work during an economic strike by their union against their employer? The U.S. Court of Appeals at Chicago found that such work was within the managerial function and accordingly enforced an NLRB decision that the union's discipline of the supervisors violated Section 8(b)(1)(B) of the Taft-Hartley Act. In rendering its decision, the court stated:

What a supervisor's proper functions are when the full complement of employees is at work under the regime of a collective bargaining agreement then in force is not determinative of supervisory responsibility during a strike . . . Insofar as the supervisors work to give the employer added economic leverage, they are acting as members of the management team are expected to act when the employer and the union are at loggerheads in their most fundamental of disputes. Indeed, in a real sense they are representing the employer for the purpose of collective bargaining, for the use of economic pressure by the parties to a labor dispute . . . is part and parcel of the process of collective bargaining. . . . Insofar as their efforts help to keep the business going in order to fulfill commitments to customers and to preserve the company's clientele and good name from deterioration, it lies at the very core of the entrepreneurial function.[91]

In another case, in early 1973, a majority of the NLRB adhered to a long-established policy by refusing to order a union to pay employees the wages lost when they were prevented from working by the union's unlawful picketing. The union began the strike against the employer in Puerto Rico on August 9, 1971. On several occasions thereafter, union agents and some of the pickets threatened a number of nonstriking employees with physical injuries and damaged some nonstrikers' cars by breaking windows and windshields and puncturing tires.

Union agents also threatened the owners of

trucks used by the employer in transporting its products, stating that the trucks would be damaged if the owners persisted in hauling the employer's products. Subsequently, shots were fired from a car belonging to one of the union agents at a tractor-trailer rig being used by the employer.

The Board's administrative-law judge found that the acts of violence and the threats attributable to the union in the course of its strike against the employer constituted restraint and coercion in violation of Section 8(b)(1)(A). He recommended that the union be ordered to cease and desist from interfering with the Section 7 rights of employees of any employer in Puerto Rico, and to mail a copy of the Board notice in English and Spanish to each employee. In addition, he recommended that the union be ordered to give back-pay to those employees who were unable to work because of its unfair labor practices.

While agreeing with the judge that the union's conduct violated Section 8(b)(1)(A), the Board majority refused to go along with the recommended back-pay order, which it described as "contrary to Board precedent." "From the earliest days of the Taft-Hartley Act," it said, "the desirability of such a remedy has been argued to the Board. In each case, the Board has refused to enlarge the scope of its traditional remedies for picket line misconduct."

In the view of the Board majority the back-pay order was "not appropriate where the union's unfair labor practices involved solely interference with an employee's right of ingress to his place of employment." The decisions embodying this view "have stood the test of 24 years of court litigation and congressional scrutiny" without being reversed or nullified.[92]

Even when a union's conduct has resulted in injury to nonunion employees or nonstrikers, the Board has limited itself to issuing a cease-and-desist order without attempting to reimburse the injured employees for loss of pay or medical expense. These damages, the Board has held, are more properly remedied by a damage action in the courts.[93]

Conclusion

Undoubtedly, there might be disagreement among union officials, management representatives, and the author as to the equities and inequities of the various conditions and situations that have been covered here. However, the real and potential harm to their institutions, and to the members of our society in general, cannot be denied. It must be apparent that the conduct and attitudes illustrated by these few cases, which are representative of thousands of others, are a profound reflection upon the state of our freedoms and rights—both corporate and union.

How can we contend that we are a free, educated, intelligent, ethical, and moral people, when such behavior is prevalent in our everyday business life and, in fact, is considered acceptable and provokes no alarm. Man's quarrelsome, aggressive, and militant nature is nowhere more evident than in labor-management relations. How much further must we evolve before we learn the wisdom and virtue in seeking only peaceful and reasonable means for resolving our differences? Or have we perhaps designed an economic system which intrinsically contains elements that make it improbable that such an objective can ever be achieved? These and so many other questions will someday have to be answered if true industrial peace is ever to be attained.

7
PREVENTING WILDCAT STRIKES

COLLECTIVE BARGAINING necessarily implies the right of the parties to disagree. But in a mature labor-management relationship, economic force, if acknowledged to be appropriate under any circumstance, should be resorted to only as an ultimate weapon and reserved for disputes which do not respond to other and more reasonable means of resolution. Its frequent and repeated use is a sign not only of unimaginativeness, but also of a considerable degree of irresponsible inflexibility in one or both parties.

There are still some leaders, in labor as well as management, who apparently believe that conflict and confrontation are the best means of obtaining equitable resolutions. The following excerpt from a United Electrical Workers Shop Steward Guide List is only one of the many possible examples of that type of thinking:

. . . when UE was first organized the established policy for the handling of grievances under the UE contract was to have grievances taken up through the grievance procedure. If no solution is found, the union and the members in the shop shall have the contractual right to engage in concerted action or strike in support of such grievance. Arbitration of a grievance could take place only if the union asked for it. This UE policy has been unique in the American trade union movement.

The contractual right to stop work over a grievance and the readiness of the workers to do so when necessary will often result in the favorable settlement of the grievance without a stoppage.

Today, Union contracts that provide for the right to stop work in support of a grievance are almost never heard of. *Too many union officials are looking for an easy way out. All they are interested in is passing the buck and to blame an arbitrator when he cuts the throat of a worker on his grievance.* Since the Taft-Hartley and Landrum-Griffin laws, *many arbitrators are daily destroying contract conditions* that workers fought for and won during the early days of industrial organization. The settlement of grievances, instead of being the job of the workers in the department and in the shop, has become the business of a whole army of lawyers, arbitrators, professors, "do-gooders" and company industrial relations men. *All of them have vested interest of their own in favor of expanding this "arbitration gas chamber" where legitimate grievances of working people are being suffocated.*

Although many UE contracts today still preserve the right to strike on grievances, and we do so when necessary, the trend to arbitration has also affected UE. UE officers and stewards must guard against this arbitration trap and must not permit arbitration to be used as a substitute for a real fight in the shop on grievances. The best place to settle a grievance is still right on the floor, at the machine and at the bench. The contractual right to strike in support of a grievance should be fought for *in every case possible,* with arbitration of a grievance only when the union asks for it. Under existing conditions a grievance should be referred to arbitration *only where the Union's case is so strong that even a brainwashed, company-minded arbitrator would have trouble ruling against the union.* In many instances, it is better to leave a grievance unsettled until the time is right to fight it out in the department than to have a company-minded arbitrator make a ruling that will scrap the contract and set a bad precedent for all future cases.

UE shop stewards and officers *must mobilize and rely on strength* of the workers they represent to settle their grievances.

We have there a sample of the strong-minded sentiment prevalent among many members of the labor-management community. It is this "might makes right" philosophy which prevails too often even in those contractual relationships which have the benefit of a firm no-strike pledge. The fact that the no-strike promise was written into the contract with the express purpose of preventing work stoppages over grievances and disputes for the duration of that contract is no guarantee that such illegal strikes will not occur.

A wildcat strike action occurs, of course, when employees resort to self-help rather than seeking redress for their complaint through the orderly processes of the contractual grievance machinery. The reasons why employees engage in such illegal work stoppages are so numerous and varied that any attempt to enumerate them all would be an exercise in futility. The issues range from the most substantive and serious to the most picayune and unbelievably absurd.

For example, at one plant the third-shift (11:00 P.M. to 7:30 A.M.) lathe and milling machine operators and all of their helpers took turns for an hour or two each night to take a nap. It was their foreman's nightly custom to go off somewhere to sleep, and the workers timed their own naps to coincide with his. They considered this reasonable, since about three-fourths of the time they would keep their machines running unattended.

A subsequent change in plant managers led to the discovery that the foreman was sleeping on the job, and he was discharged. When the workers were advised that thereafter they would stay awake or be subject to discipline and perhaps even discharge, they walked out in violation of the contract's no-strike clause. Their object was to preserve their "hard-won" working condition and to write into the contract their right to catch 40 winks on the third shift.

When the first-shift employees reported to work the next morning, they refrained from entering the plant. However, most of those several hundred people did not know why they were not going to work. Three days later, when the employees were finally induced to come back to work, many asked their foreman why they had been on strike—for they still did not know—and when they were told did not believe the foreman.

It is now up to the reader to place that issue on

a scale ranging from the substantive to the absurd, and to judge for himself the present state of maturity of our labor-management game and its players.

However, no matter what the reason for a wildcat strike, it is safe to say that the best way to stop it is to prevent it from starting in the first place. And sometimes management can play an important role in such prevention.

Employees naturally tend to look, consciously or not, to their employer as at least one source of counsel or information in evaluating the merits of two competing choices. It is this fundamental condition which may make it possible for an alert management representative to nip an imminent illegal activity in the bud. Granted, the odds are not great that he will suceed in preventing a work stoppage, but the potential reward is great enough to justify the effort. And even when unsuccessful, that effort can provide management with (1) meaningful information as to causes, motivations, participation, and leadership and (2) evidence of worker-worker or worker-union cohesion or division.

PEACEKEEPING IDEAS FOR MANAGEMENT

In the imminent wildcat situation the supervisor on the floor is most often the management man in the middle. Although this is not an uncommon place to find himself in—it is precisely where he is day in and day out—he is in fact now facing a most uncommon situation. A threatening wildcat strike places unusual demands on a supervisor's leadership abilities and resources. Therefore, it is wise to advise the supervisor of the conduct management hopes to obtain from him should the need arise. The following subsections are designed to improve the supervisor's ability to prevent or mitigate a work stoppage in his area by (1) providing facts that he should be aware of and (2) suggesting measures he can take if and when a stoppage occurs.

Understanding the Nature of Strikes

Strikes and slowdowns by their very nature are concerted actions. *Webster's New Collegiate Dictionary* defines concerted as "mutually contrived or agreed on" or "performed in unison." Certainly mutuality and unison are not attainable by an individual acting alone but require two or more persons performing together. If a single employee refuses to work, or walks out, or slows down, his actions may be appropriately described as insubordinate or in violation of shop rules. Violation of a contract's no-strike article, however, can be attributed only to two or more—and most often it is many more than two—employees acting in concert.

This is a very important concept for the supervisor to understand, for it makes him aware that a wildcat strike cannot take place without some planning—whether hasty or thorough—by its participants. They could not act in unison without some degree of planning.

Therefore, among the participating employees there will be someone who had the initial idea, who either suggested, proposed, or urged it. There will be other members of the group who urged that the illegal action be taken, and later may even have openly demonstrated their leadership initiative. Also among the group will be those who will go along with whatever the majority decided, irrespective of their own attitudes about it, and there may be other members who are very opposed. Realizing all of this may prepare the foreman to be more alert to any outward signs of preparation for a strike and also enable him to interpret more correctly what he may see or hear.

Awareness of Union Foreknowledge

In the majority of cases, the wildcat strike arises out of prior discussions leading to advance planning and ultimate execution. More often than not, one or more union representatives will have prior knowledge of the employees' plans, except where the situation arises from spontaneous combustion. The smaller the establishment, the greater is the likelihood that more than one union representative will have advance knowledge.

Despite the size of the establishment, it is more than likely that one or more union representatives—such as a department steward, an area or district committeeman, or the like—are located in the department or plant area where the stoppage begins. In most cases (nonspontaneous combustion), such union representatives have previously participated in a discussion with management of the grievance, complaint, discipline action, change in working conditions, or the like, which was later to result in the employees' self-help actions. As a worker himself, the local union representative works among employees and hears them discussing such matters and expressing attitudes, feelings, and reactions. While he may not be an actual party to the self-help plan, it is doubtful that he is not at least aware of it.

The fact that union representatives have had prior knowledge of a wildcat strike or have participated as planners is not impossible to establish while it may be quite difficult. Because they are generally aware of the consequences of their involvement, if it is proven, self-interest will naturally impel them to disclaim it. Awareness of the potential role of union representatives can help supervisors to sharpen their interpretations of what they see and hear both before and during a wildcat incident.

Observing and Recording Illegal Actions

The management will need facts for documentation. These are obtained primarily from the supervisor's observations: Everything of importance that he sees and hears and his reasonable inferences and deductions based on those observations should be recorded promptly and opportunely. Accordingly, he should *not* leave the work area where the self-help action is developing or taking place. He cannot see, hear, or record what happens during his absence.

Also, if he leaves this battleground, he forfeits whatever affirmative leadership he might otherwise have brought to bear in opposition to the self-help action. He should be in plain view of the employee participants, so they are aware of his presence and his attendant ability to see, hear, and report on their conduct and behavior.

It is hoped that his presence will help to deter the employees from continuing their peace-disturbing conduct; but if that should fail, he is still in a position to record, and later to report, what took place. Realization that he can do so may in itself deter employees who do not strongly support the illegal action or who do not wish to jeopardize their jobs over the issue involved.

To obtain pertinent facts the foreman should be alert and observant. He should ask himself the following questions:

How many employees can I recognize and identify?

Where are they standing or sitting, and what are they doing?

Are there any union stewards or committeemen or officers among them—or are they conspicuous by their absence?

Informing Your Superiors

Naturally more than one observer would be beneficial. But again, it is unwise for the supervisor to create a leadership vacuum by leaving the area of the action to seek help or to inform others. However, if a telephone is in the immediate area and can be used so that he retains a good view of the employees, and they of him, he may wish to briefly advise the industrial relations man, the plant manager, or even his immediate superior of the problem. Sometimes the presence of a still-higher management authority who is recognized as such by employees will permit stronger persuasion or greater deterrence.

There is still another approach which has occasionally been helpful: In advance, the supervisor might select a reliable person as a messenger to get word to higher management personnel in the event of a wildcat situation. He may have some nonunion salaried individual who works regularly in his area, such as a time-study man, a quality assurance inspector, an expediter, a records or timekeeping clerk, a payroll clerk, or any number of others in this category. In the face of such an emergency, he could then go direct to this selected individual and send him with an appropriate message.

However, if that avenue is not open to him, for whatever reason, he may try still another approach. It is possible—and only the particular situation can dictate the probability of success—he may have among the hourly workers an individual who, *under certain circumstances,* would accede to carrying a message for him to another management member. Presumably the person is mature, reasonable, and sensible and is unlikely to participate in conduct which violates the labor agreement.

If the foreman chooses to pursue this course of action, he must realize the awkward social position in which such a messenger would be placed. He could not ask this person to deliver the message *as a favor* to him or to the company. Perhaps the best (if not the only) approach for the foreman is to issue a direct order to this potential messenger in order to relieve him of personal responsibility. For example, "I am giving you a direct order: Go to Mr. _____ and tell him I have an emergency in my department and want him to come here immediately. Then return directly to me and report the outcome."

If the supervisor meets with any resistance, he can further relieve that person of social responsibility by making the order even firmer: "Look, I've given you a reasonable order which I expect to have carried out. If you fail, or if you refuse, you may be subjecting yourself to discipline for insubordination." This is certainly not the most desirable alternative, but neither is the situation desirable in which the foreman finds himself; and by its very nature, that situation does not provide a multitude of alternatives for the foreman.

Sending Strikers Home?

A serious mistake commonly made by supervisors who find themselves in this situation is to tell the employees, who are probably milling around indecisively, "Go to work or go home." The employees can then choose to interpret such an order as giving them an option, and more often than not they will opt to go home. Such an order may even be so interpreted by an arbitrator who judges it later, usually after the company has disciplined any employees who did leave the premises.

Presumably management wants all participating employees to go back to work. Therefore, it is not in the foreman's best interests to issue an order which provides the employees with a choice which could result in an unwanted consequence. In fact, it is inadvisable to send anyone home. After others have walked out, some employees, and often these will be union representatives, will say, "Well, I may as well go along home too. Without the rest of the crew, you don't need me, so there's no sense in my finishing out my shift." (This might be called nonparticipating participation in a work stoppage.) An experienced foreman will generally reply, "No, I'm not granting you permission to leave during working hours. There is work I can provide for you to do, and I want you to stay and do it. And, further, I expect you to return at the start of your next shift of work."

If he meets resistance, he becomes a little firmer, saying something in the nature of, "I am not granting permission for you to leave. I'm now giving you a direct order to (do a particular task, reasonable and appropriate). I don't want to take disciplinary action for insubordination, but I will if you make such action unavoidable."

To summarize, in this situation, most experienced foremen will provide only two choices: the employee can either go back to work or be disciplined. To those who argue that they are no longer needed, the foreman will stress that work *is* available, that no permission to go home is therefore being granted, and that refusal to stay and work will result in disciplinary action.

Types of Self-Help Actions

Violations of the no-strike clause can take a myriad of unusual forms. An all-encompassing list would be prohibitively long, but a few of the more common forms include:

> Staying at machines or equipment but not working.
>
> Remaining seated at lunch tables beyond the lunch hour.
>
> Milling about in rest rooms when work should be resumed.
>
> Shutting down machines when they normally would be operating.
>
> Leaving work stations and gathering up personal belongings.

Of course, there are many forms of concerted activity over which a foreman may exercise little, if any, control. However, the few activities listed were chosen because they are typical of employee group actions over which a foreman may provide effective persuasion.

Enlisting the Union Representative's Aid

If a union representative is present when the illegal stoppage occurs, perhaps it is advisable to go directly to him and ask what is wrong and why the employees are not working. Perhaps the representative should be asked to suggest to his constituents that they are doing wrong and should return to work. If he refuses, he should explain why he has done so. The foreman may request that the steward (or other representative) accompany him as he goes from man to man inquiring:

Why are you not working?
Who told you to stop work?
Do you intend to return to work?
Are you having any trouble with your machine, equipment, materials, tools? If so, go to your work station and I'll have that condition remedied.

During these engagements, the foreman should be mentally recording who said what, whether there was a particular spokesman and what he said or did, and what the union representative said or did.

In the presence of the workers, he may direct these questions to the steward:

What they are doing is wrong, isn't it?
They can be disciplined or discharged for this, can't they?
You're not going to join in this too, are you?
You're going to go back to work, aren't you?

(See the discussion of "negative leadership" by union officers in Chapter 5.)

Some Important Points

Throughout all of this the foreman's demeanor is of the utmost importance. He should not be pugnacious, overly aggressive, militaristic, loud, profane, or at all emotional. He must be calm, cool, as unperturbable as possible, and firm but not dictatorial.

During his brief questioning of each man, or of

the group collectively, there are three last essential remarks which must be made, that follow hand in glove with the initial inquiries. In essence they are:

1. *Whatever* your complaint is, I will meet with your representatives and discuss it *as soon as* you've all returned to work. I will *not* delay or postpone that meeting, it will be held *immediately after* you've all returned to work.

2. I'm going to give you a direct order to resume working. (This is preferably said to each individual, but if dictated otherwise by the situation, can be said to the group collectively.) We can resolve our problem without this action of yours being necessary.

3. Do you realize the consequences of your action if you continue with it? You are each subjecting yourselves to severe discipline and perhaps to loss of employment. The union may be liable for a damage suit if you go through with this. I'm directing you again to return to your jobs and resume working.

It is important at this point to take particular note of all individual reactions, remarks, and gestures. If the foreman's efforts have failed, in whole or in part, it is still important to notice who demonstrates leadership aimed either at a return to work or at carrying the self-help action further. All employees are not equally guilty, and some may not be at all. It is more important to identify the leaders or instigators if possible. Identifying their complaint is equally essential.

It is highly inadvisable to agree to discuss the workers' complaint and bring it to a resolution while they persist in withholding their labor. This can be only a shortcut to longer-range labor difficulties. If management submits while the gun is at its head, so to speak, it is inviting that gun to be so placed over and over again. It may well lead to a substitution of the peaceful and orderly contractual grievance procedure by chaotic self-help remedies. But if there has been enough heat generated by the employees' complaint, whatever it is, to provoke them to mob behavior, management will be shortsighted and foolish if it does not provide a good-faith hearing on the matter *as soon as* they are working again.

As soon as the dust has settled, the management principals who were directly engaged in the work stoppage should immediately, while it is all still fresh in their minds, record everything they have seen or heard. This should then be placed in the hands of the proper higher-management authority.

The recommendations put forth here are clearly and certainly not anti-employee or anti-union. They are intended purely to restore order and peaceful labor relations. It may be argued that management should not let matters get to this explosive stage in the first place. If the explosive condition was caused or contributed to by management, that goes without saying. But this book sadly recognizes the reality of the existence of conflict. At the same time it is concerned with suggesting measures which can be employed to restore peace and provide industrial justice. It was solely for that purpose that this section has been put forth.

UNDERSTANDING YOUR UNION

In a mass society, according to one theory, man does not look to God or to himself for his salvation or for his way of life, but rather to other people. It is often said that all of us are mesmerized by our television sets, view the same movies, wear the same kinds of clothes, make similar decisions, and in general do the same things. We are living in a carbon-copy culture, with the print growing paler and paler as we all repeat what others do, until finally the last trace of carbon disappears and only blankness (boredom) is left.

Our educational system, with its emphasis upon conformity; our families who try to fit us into accepted roles; our economic system, which critics say tends to develop organization men; our religions, which frequently provide houses for social gatherings instead of houses of prayer; our political system, in which it is difficult to find new ideas put forth by any leader able to implement them; our peer groups, which put pressure on members to behave alike—all these agencies of our society have made us, if our critics are right, "other-directed," to use David Reisman's phrase. More and more, we employ as standards of judgment what others think, rather than what we think, is right. In fact, perhaps imperceptibly, what others think becomes what we think.[94]

The Political Orientation of the Union

One of the groups most affected by such pressures for conformity is the union membership, composed of employees who feel a compelling need to identify with others in the group. The union's representatives are sensitive to these conditions and are ever alert to ways they can more satisfactorily meet the needs of the employees.

Frequently, the union's representatives are well-informed and highly dedicated individuals whose primary interest is effective representation of their membership. But basically, the union's officers and representatives must continue to satisfy the needs of their constituents, or at least appear to be making every effort to do so, if they are to be re-elected. Politically, the union representative holds his position at the pleasure of his work group, and unless he is responsive to it, his future in the union can be jeopardized.

In many factories, responsible union officials are sensitive to the need for reasonable grievance adjudication and the need to remove all internal roadblocks that cause friction or failures. However, far too often internal union politics, manifesting itself in numerous forms, interferes with or prevents the orderly and responsible settlement of grievance disputes.

The sophisticated manager recognizes that, irrespective of the particular bent of its officials, the union is basically an institution with certain political motivations. Its needs are many and varied but can usually be placed into four general categories:

1. To perpetuate itself, the union must always seek "more" for its members. "More" may be additional wages, improved benefits, better working conditions, fewer hours without reduced income, and so forth.

2. It must constantly strive to increase membership since dues from employees constitute its source of income, its lifeblood. It must therefore invariably contest any management effort to make any change resulting in fewer workers.

3. It must always try to improve its own economic status, and this may be accomplished in a variety of ways. It commonly seeks company payment of union time for grievance processing and investigations and for a myriad of other union activities attendant upon administration of the labor agreement. By so doing, it acts to reduce the drain on its own economic resources.

4. It must always be "competitive." The needs and desires of its membership must be met—or at least the members must feel that their union is doing everything in its power to satisfy those needs. Unless this is happening, the union may lose the workers' loyalty to one of those unions that are constantly suggesting to organized workers that they can represent them more effectively than the incumbent organization.

Role of the Union Representative

In labor-management relations there is no room for prejudice toward union representatives. The presence of the union organization in the plant effects a labor-management marriage and a corresponding obligation to observe the vows of recognition and good faith.

In their grievance relationship, for example, the foreman and steward are coequals. They are also subject to similar pressures. The steward is expected to keep apprised of plant rules, bonus systems, safety regulations, time-study matters, job evaluation plans, pension plans, labor law developments, and procedures of discipline.

The foreman, because of his close relationship with the workers and their problems, feels a closeness and a kinship with them that most other management representatives do not share. As a member of the management, and as its spokesman and advocate, he may sometimes find his own personal feelings toward the issue in conflict with the management position he must endorse. The steward faces a similar problem. His close association with the employees subjects him to certain group pressures and thinking to which he, as an individual and an employee, may not personally subscribe.

All of these elements and factors are present when these two advocates come together. Each has a job to do and should be performing it in the manner that best serves the interests of his institution, as well as the mutual interests of both organizations. To effectively accomplish their joint purpose, each party must treat the other with due respect. Obviously, the company and the union have met on equal terms and adopted a contract recognizing each other's rights. Now each has its dignity and purpose to uphold. Organizations and corporations can act only through agents and representatives. To the extent that each treats the other with respect and recognition, their joint problems will be resolved more effectively and to their mutual satisfaction.

When the shop steward contemplates the limitations and requirements within which he must function, he may see himself as merely responding to a variety of pressures and demands with little choice and ineffectual powers. On the one hand, he is pushed by the demands of an electorate he must satisfy or suffer a damaging loss of popularity; on the other hand, he frequently finds himself dealing with a management apparently deaf to his arguments and needs. The steward is more likely to feel this way when management views the labor agreement as representing the sum total of what has been given and all that there is to be gained by him and the union.

The union representative actually functions in a dual capacity. On the one hand, he is usually a bargaining-unit employee who has some hourly productive job requiring the performance of a certain set of duties and functions. When functioning in this capacity, he naturally is governed by the same rules and regulations of behavior and conduct that apply to other unit employees, such as those for attendance, lateness, output, effort, and so on. On the other hand, when in the role of union representative, he dons a cloak that provides him with *a certain degree* of immunity, and his conduct and behavior are measured by a different yardstick. As an advocate for his special interest group, he must enjoy a certain latitude in vigorously representing his constituents and carrying out the necessary duties of his office.

However, that immunity and latitude do not apply to the union representative in his role as employee, as illustrated by the following case brought before an arbitrator: The outdoor work of some 30 to 40 men was halted for about an hour because of rain, and when the rain markedly slackened, the supervisor signaled the men to return to work. All of them did so except the union official, who remained under the shelter and made no attempt whatever to discuss the matter with his foreman. In deciding this matter, the arbitrator commented:

Quite aside from rejecting the grievant's belated and self-serving effort to explain away his behavior by saying he had put on his union hat as the General Foreman approached, the Umpire believes that it should also be noted that X's status as a Shop Steward did not, in any event, mean that he was immune from the obligation to obey reasonable orders by his supervisor to return to work. . . .[95]

The Management Viewpoint

It is well to remember that the union is often influenced by political considerations and that political factions may spring up and develop among workers. In any event, seldom are politically inspired grievances reconcilable by the first-line supervisor. The motivation and forces at work behind such grievances preclude an early resolution of the dispute. The grievants and/or the union in such situations usually are predetermined to press the matter all the way—unless the company completely submits to their claim.

The typical manager is accustomed to basing his management decisions primarily on economic considerations and to dealing with other like-minded company executives. He may not understand why unions are not similarly motivated. It may be difficult for him to rationalize why the union takes certain apparently illogical positions, engaging in the grandstand appeals and pressure tactics more commonly associated with the politician. The fact is that the value judgments of the union do not always place economic considerations at the top, as do the overwhelming majority of management decisions.

The solution for the embattled management is not to wrestle with or complain about these unalterable factors, but instead attempt to understand the motivation of the union steward and the political orientation of the institution he serves. By its nature, the union is not a secure organization, and its manners are typically militant and highly suspicious and ofttimes emotionally charged.

The security of the union organization is wholly dependent upon its acting in a way to prove its worth and merit to the membership. Repeatedly, the union representative will seek to have the benefits that accrue to the worker come through in such a manner as to secure, maintain, and reinforce the worker's union loyalty. Management can do little to prevent such manifestations of union policy. But it can do much to fortify and clarify its own position with the workers if it learns to recognize the union's motivation for what it is and to deal with it realistically.

8
ALTERNATIVES to the STRIKE

ON FEBRUARY 1, 1974, *The Wall Street Journal* reported that strikes by independent truckers had forced the closedown of one steel plant and the imminent closedown of another, both in eastern Ohio. About 750 workers were laid off at one of the plants, the Martins Ferry plant of the Wheeling-Pittsburgh Steel Corporation. At the other, the Youngstown Sheet and Tube Company's Campbell plant, near Youngstown, about 1,000 workers were soon to be idled. *The Wall Street Journal* also reported disrupted operations at other plants in the East and Midwest.

On February 3, 1974, the Associated Press reported more layoffs as the truckers' shutdown spread further over more than 20 states, prompting federal officials to ask the nation's governors to restore peace and commerce to the highways. Reports of scattered violence increased, and shutdowns had by then idled more than 10,000 workers.

Potential food shortages became a major worry as shippers of produce reported sharp drops in truck movements, and at least a dozen meat-packing plants and slaughterhouses reported they had closed or curtailed operations.

The story unfolded further on February 4, 1974, when the Associated Press reported additional developments. By this date the truckers' strike had idled over 20,000 workers in affected industries and further crippled deliveries of meat and produce in some areas.

Officials in 15 states reported shootings, rock throwing, and tire and hose slashings over the prior weekend. Two drivers suffered shoulder wounds from bullets which struck their trucks near New Buffalo, Michigan, and Louisville, Kentucky. A Pennsylvania official said there had been 14 shootings at trucks and up to 100 other violent incidents since the strike had started four days before. One trucker died in the violence. About 3,400 National Guardsmen now stood watch on Ohio and Pennsylvania highways.

The dispute had by now touched 30 states, from Connecticut to Florida, across the South and Midwest and along the southwest border of the country from Texas to California. Governors officially deplored the continuing violence. U.S. Attorney General William B. Saxbe said, "This handful of truckers is not going to bring this country to its knees."

An immediate concern was food. By this point

an estimated 20 meat-packing plants in Iowa, Michigan, Oklahoma, Texas, and Pennsylvania were closed or cutting back operations, idling at least another 8,000 workers.

The number of involved drivers could not be determined. One truckers' spokesman said 90,000 of the country's estimated 100,000 independents were staying off the road. Some other union drivers also were not moving, mostly because they feared violence.

By February 7, 1974, most of the nation's newspapers were carrying daily headlines of the strike and its effects. Fuel supplies were being strangled, school systems were closing around the country, and some cities were gasless.

Another trucker was killed, shot on a Delaware road, and countless others displayed bullet holes in their rigs. West Virginia Governor Arch A. Moore, Jr., ordered armed National Guard troops to ride in each truck in the five counties of his state that were hardest hit by the shutdown.

By this time, more than 75,000 layoffs had been reported, and in the auto industry alone, more than 26,000 workers were off the job in Wisconsin, Ohio, Illinois, Missouri, and Indiana because of parts shortages.

By February 8 the continuing shutdown had left at least 100,000 persons jobless and some regions dangerously short of critical supplies. Stretches of the nation's highways were under heavy guard as violence spread even further. Extra police patrols were ordered at critical areas in ten states and National Guard units were on duty in seven states. Someone attempted to dynamite a bridge on the Pennsylvania Turnpike, at least ten states reported shootings and rock throwings, and Pittsburgh police said 50 men broke into the headquarters of a steel haulers group and attempted to start a fire.

The American Meat Institute, based in Chicago, said that if the strike was not settled by the weekend, two days away, nearly all meat-packers and processors would be forced to close, idling about 250,000 workers. An Illinois chamber of commerce official said if the strike were to continue another week, half a million workers in his state might be laid off.

On the next day, troopers in Kentucky arrested four more truck drivers on charges of carrying arms. On the previous day, this law enforcement department had arrested four drivers and confiscated several pistols, a rifle, a switchblade knife, and two boxes of ammunition. All of the guns were loaded.

The situation had become so critical by February 9 that President Richard M. Nixon took to the airwaves to elaborate on the transportation measures he was proposing. The broadcast came live from the White House and was carried by all three major news networks: ABC, CBS, and NBC. In the meantime, negotiations in Washington continued at a feverish pace in marathon sessions.

On February 11 a compromise settlement was finally hammered out, and though many drivers were still dissatisfied and sporadic incidents of violence continued to occur at various places across the country, the back of the issue seemed to have been broken. In the week that followed, things slowly returned to normalcy.

But, the fusillades of rifle fire, barrages of rocks, trip-hammer sluggings, and shafts of flame on the nation's highways may have merely been a preview of many coming attractions. Not the least of which could be a repeat performance by these same independent truckers.

However, should the long-time dream of the Teamster's Union ever be realized, it may easily lead us all to what could aptly be titled: "The Day the United States Stood Still." That long-time dream turns on something called by labor relations practitioners "the common expiration date of all such union contracts."

As it was, the only thing that prevented that worse horror story in February, 1974, was that the independents were not really centrally organized, being fragmented by ambitious local leaders. Were that the case, as it may well be the next time around, they too would be a force powerful enough to disrupt billions of dollars worth of commerce, industry, and employment.

The problems related to strikes such as the independents carried out are ever ongoing. By no means did the problems of that particular strike stop on February 11 with the beginning of the end of the strike. The following is an excerpt from a United Press International story carried on February 14, 1974, relating an incident that occurred at Lansing, Michigan:

Angry picket line tradesmen smashed windows, slashed tires and tipped over two flatbed trucks on a nonunion construction project Wednesday and then invaded a restaurant owned by the contractor and "tore the place apart."

The violence started early in the day at a construction site where a trucker employed by a subcontractor drove his rig into picketers Tuesday, injuring nine persons, one seriously.

A group of about 50 men left the picket line Wednesday and marched some two blocks to Long's Restaurant, walked in and began tearing up seats and smashing light fixtures while customers watched.

Damage was estimated at $10,000 by the restaurant owner, Gordon L. Long, who also is the main contractor on the construction project. Long was in seclusion following a reported beating on the job site Tuesday and several threats on his life and those of his family. . . .[96]

Are Strikes Inevitable?

Thus again we see the true dimensions of peaceful coexistence in the labor-management community. Again the question must be asked: Is collective bargaining working as well as civilized people can make it, when such as this are its by-products and results?

When labor unions are weak, employer-labor disputes are localized and affect relatively few persons. When there are strong unions in the important base industries, their conflicts with employers can disturb the general economy and affect the well-being of the entire nation, and even of foreign countries. Thus, the stronger and more active the labor movement in a key industry becomes, the greater is the need to find means to avoid work stoppages.

But before the search for solutions can begin, the parties themselves must recognize that such a need exists. And, they must also believe that strikes are *not* inevitable.

When is a fact a fact? In the labor-management (economic) world, few premises like "*All* things are this way," or "This is *always* thus and so" can be justified. Such statements are called universal propositions. It is important to recognize that a universal proposition can never be completely validated by evidence. We can never examine all the cases to find out whether it was always true in the past, but even more important, we can never be sure that it will always be true in the future, even if it has always been true in the past.

The belief that strikes are inevitable is a prime example of a universal proposition, and yet parties in collective bargaining often fallaciously accept that proposition as an irrefutable fact. How many times has it been said that the strike is the union's *only* means for achieving its objectives, and each time that statement is repeated, such a belief is reinforced in the minds of speakers and listeners alike—thus increasingly dimming the hope that a more enlightened means will ever be attempted.

We need to be especially careful about extending the "facts" of the past into the future, unless we are confident that our conclusions are irrefutable and the circumstances that produced the facts are unchangeable. We must get used to the idea that what we accept as facts are seldom absolute—that "almost always true" or maybe only "60 percent true" is not the same as "always true."

OBSTACLES TO ECONOMIC PEACE

The fact that strikes are not inevitable does not mean that avoiding them is an easy task. Collective bargaining is a process of challenge and response. It includes innumerable variations as individual companies and unions shape it to fit their needs. For the most part it settles the disputes between employers and unions. But sometimes they cannot, or will not, reach agreement.

The issues at stake in labor negotiations are seldom simple. The quarrel that the public sees in the newspapers is often only part of the real issue. The fine speeches made by both sides—about the need for wage increases to fight the rising cost of living, or the need to protect against inflationary prices and further erosion of profits—sound good on news broadcasts but often have little to do with settling the dispute at the bargaining table. To look at the issues in terms of a simple dollars-and-cents comparison is naive.

There are few more complex jobs of compromise and good human relations than labor-management negotiations. The issues are real, and no purpose is served by pretending that nothing is involved but the common interests of the parties. Unfortunately, there is seldom a clear, objective answer.

Maintaining industrial peace is especially difficult when the parties involved in a controversy are approximately equal in bargaining strength. Some see further legislation as the means to eliminating strikes and lockouts. However, because of the nature of the problem they attempt to remedy, laws to discourage or prohibit work stoppages must restrict certain actions of workers and their unions. Will such laws thereby tip the scale in favor of employers, and ultimately destroy the equilibrium necessary for effective collective bargaining?

In considering the causes of industrial disputes, the inherent disadvantageous position of workers in relation to their employers and the public must ever be kept in mind. Employers are able to improve their economic condition—that is, increase their profits—without consulting their employees or inconveniencing the public by lockouts. Workers cannot improve or even maintain their existing standards without the approval of their employer; and if he refuses to raise the standards or insists on lowering them, the generally adopted recourse has been to strike.

A few employers can meet quietly in a New York office and decide upon a labor policy which will affect hundreds of thousands of workers. The public may never know of their concerted action, but it is well aware of any concerted action by the employees when they protest the working conditions resulting from this agreed-upon policy because such protests must be carried on in the open.

The inherent inequality in the strategies available to employers and workers must always be kept in mind in any consideration of laws to bring about "equality" in the employer-employee relationship. This chapter, however, is concerned not primarily with the rights of employers versus those of workers but rather with a consideration of the means available for protecting the general welfare against the impact of disputes between the two groups. Because these disputes stem from varied causes and circumstances, there can be no generalization about methods for handling all of them. The remedies and methods for mitigating their effects upon the public, whether by law or private arrangement, must be fitted to the circumstances attending the various kinds of disputes. The proposed remedies must also take into consideration the merits and deficiencies of alternative measures.

Therefore, the following remedies—which have worked for some parties, and in one instance for an entire nation—should not be construed as panaceas but as vehicles for ideas that can possibly be adapted to specific needs. Above all, these alternatives are meant to convey hope to labor-management adversaries—the hope that they too can learn to resolve their problems without recourse to the strike and lockout.

DETERRING THE STRIKE

Free collective bargaining—that is, the opportunity for labor and management to work out their own problems and to arrive at voluntary agreement concerning them—is an essential element of economic democracy. Indeed, it is today, as it has been for at least a quarter-century, our declared national labor policy. Although the government considers it important to minimize interruptions of operations, it has continually recognized the right of employers and unions to reject a proffered agreement, even at the expense of such interruptions.

In free collective bargaining the objective is voluntary agreement arrived at through the process of reasoning and persuasion. In order to work, collective bargaining requires that the parties reconcile their separate interests and bring them into line with those of the public—that is, that they seriously attempt to eliminate, or at least reduce the scope of, avoidable interruptions of operations.

As time has moved on, one might expect to see less of the hostility which characterized collective bargaining in its early stages, and a greater degree of social responsibility. Yes, there have been improvements, but not of the consequence one should reasonably expect after almost half a century. In suggesting wider use of the improved procedures discussed in the following subsections, what is sought is to have collective bargaining become more effective and responsible so that it may remain free.

The Dunbar Furniture Strike Work Agreement

This agreement was negotiated by the Dunbar Furniture Corporation of Berne, Indiana, and the Upholsterers' International Union of North

America (affiliated with the AFL-CIO) acting through its agency, Upholsterers' Furniture and Wood Workers' Local Union No. 222. Made in May 1964, the strike work agreement was amended about a year later and reaffirmed in 1968. It was still in effect at this writing. The agreement is intended to permit production as usual during a labor dispute through an unusual set of financial arrangements which make it desirable for the parties to settle the matter as promptly as possible. The theory behind the agreement is that some customers are lost permanently to other suppliers during a strike or lockout, with resulting loss to both the company and the employees.

When the collective bargaining agreement expires and the union decides to strike or the company decides to stage a lockout, it must send official written notice of its decision to the other party. As outlined in the strike work agreement, the strike work procedure goes into effect on the first payroll week after the notice is received. The agreement operates as follows (for a complete copy of this agreement, see Appendix 6):

The collective bargaining contract is reinstated and continues in force for the entire strike work period, and all employees continue to work.

One-third of the earnings of each employee in the unit is withheld and placed each week in the strike work trust fund in the custody of the bank named in the fiduciary agreement. An amount equal to the total paid by the employees is placed in the fund each week by the company. The employees' and company's money is refundable in whole or in part, depending on how soon the strike work is settled. If the strike work is settled within:

The first period—four weeks—all of the money is returned to the employees and the company. The bank will donate its services.

The second period—two weeks—75 percent of the money will be returned to the employees and the company, less 10¢ per check issued in the distribution process.

The third period—one week—50 percent of the money is returned to the employees and the company, less 10¢ per check issued in the distribution process.

The fourth period—one week—25 percent of the money will be returned to the employees and the company, less 10¢ per check issued in the distribution process.

If the strike work has not been settled by the end of the fourth period (eighth week), no money will be refunded. The strike work agreement and the collective bargaining agreement may then be terminated and an "old-fashioned" (their words) strike or lockout may be initiated by written notice from the acting party. If no such notice has been received by either party by the end of the ninth week after the strike work started, then the last labor agreement will be automatically renewed without change for one year.

Any money remaining in the fund at the end of the strike work cannot be used for the benefit of the company, the employees, or the union but may be donated to a project or projects for the general good of citizens of Berne, Indiana, and its vicinity. How the beneficiaries of such donations are determined is further particularized in the parties' fiduciary agreement.

Here then is an interesting example of the innovation and ingenuity of two parties and their evident determination to avoid impasse and confrontation. Though the strike work agreement still allows for a strike or lockout, it makes that eventuality unlikely and even more undesirable than it normally is. The strike work agreement certainly contains elements that provide economic motivation for agreeing rather than disagreeing. The penalties are real and equal for both parties, and both benefit equally if agreement is reached.

Last-Offer Arbitration

Labor-management relationships, unlike those between husbands and wives, cannot be severed. Sooner or later, however bitter the dispute, the employees must work and the employer must have them return to work. It is no answer to suggest that individuals may elect to seek another place of employment; the employee body must remain. A few defections will not change the character of the problems of the body.

The economic tests of strength are no more than demonstrations of who can stand misery and suffering longer. There is little relevance to the merits of either position. Power and force cannot be transformed into morality or justice.

185

Concomitant with the right to resort to economic force is the obligation to exercise that right responsibly, sparingly, and only when no other means of arriving at settlements are feasible. Because of the inevitable losses and economic deprivations entailed in many strikes and lockouts, parties to a collective bargaining relationship owe it to themselves and the public to delimit the use of these weapons to the greatest extent possible.

The purpose of collective bargaining as protected by the National Labor Relations Act is to reduce and eliminate strikes in industry. Any further steps in that direction should be welcomed instead of discouraged.

Perhaps the utilization of voluntary arbitration as a terminal negotiating facility is one significant method of achieving this end. The overwhelming majority of parties recognize and accept the desirability of waiving the strike or lockout in favor of voluntary arbitration *during* a contract term, and neither union nor management has disappeared or been weakened by the adoption of that means of settling disputes. On the contrary, both parties are strengthened by avoiding the danger of strikes during the contract term.

Nor would unions and management disintegrate if there were some form of arbitral arrangement for terminal issues in negotiations. Each side could do yeoman service for its constituents in presenting their arguments to the arbitrator and getting as much as possible through this terminal arbitration.

It is regrettable that more disputants who see

the value of grievance arbitration do not also recognize arbitration's potential for the settlement of negotiation disputes and the avoidance of work-stopping confrontations. In negotiation disputes, management seems to feel unwilling to trust the judgment of an outsider who has no responsibility for conducting the business. Labor in turn seems to feel that giving up its opportunity to strike and relying on an outsider involves too large a risk. This is ironic since during a contract's term both parties frequently place their trust in and reliance on such outsiders, allowing them to determine matters of far-reaching consequence.

How Last-Offer Arbitration Works. A simple but dramatic form of last-offer arbitration is now being used by the Major League Baseball Players Association and the major league club owners. Under their new system, a player who cannot reach a contract agreement with his club may choose to submit the dispute to one of 14 arbitrators. The system is voluntary, however, and the player may, if he wishes, continue negotiating.

If he chooses arbitration, he and the club each name a final salary figure and submit arguments and evidence to support the merit of that particular salary to the arbitrator, who then must choose either one or the other. The arbitrator may not decide on a compromise figure or on any other figure different from the two submitted.

In 1974, when the system was introduced, a total of 45 players submitted their salary dispute to an arbitrator. In that year, for example, an arbitrator awarded Reggie Jackson of the Oakland Athletics an annual salary of $135,000. Jackson had been selected as the American League's Most Valuable Player for 1973, when his estimated salary was $70,000. The Oakland club owner, Charles O. Finley, had offered Jackson $100,000 for 1974, but the player felt that his past year's performance merited the $135,000 figure and the arbitrator agreed.

Advantages of Last-Offer Arbitration. Granted that the foregoing is a rather simplistic example of last-offer arbitration, and that the issues which the industrial scene presents to an arbitrator are likely to be more diverse and complex. But the principle remains the same, as do the long-range beneficial effects of the process on *both* parties. In fact, on comparing a strike settlement with a settlement by last-offer arbitration in terms of their overall effects on labor, management, *and* the public, the scales tip heavily in favor of arbitration.

Though particularized information is not readily available, the author is of the opinion that —except for total victory by either side, which is infrequent—the final settlements arrived at after a long, drawn-out strike are *not* far apart from the terminal positions of both parties. Had the unresolved issues precipitating the strike been submitted to an arbiter, the parties more than likely would have concluded an agreement about the same, if not in fact the same, as the one which cost them millions of dollars and misery and suffering to everyone concerned.

Where the parties voluntarily agree to submit to last-offer arbitration when a bargaining impasse results, they realize that the arbitrator has the authority to choose between their respective proposals. Both parties are thereby motivated to put forth their most equitable, most justifiable, and most reasonable proposal. Furthermore, the knowledge that arbitration awaits them should they fail to reach agreement can provide the parties with the incentive to work out their problems beforehand.

Terminal Arbitration in the Steel Industry. A hopeful sign in the use of arbitration as a means of settling collective bargaining disputes is the 1973 agreement between the United Steelworkers Union and the nation's ten biggest steel producers. Under this agreement the union relinquished the right to call a national strike in return for a guaranteed minimum 3 percent wage increase plus a one-time $150 bonus for every worker.

The more relevant matter here is the provision that all unresolved issues in the national negotiations are to go to binding arbitration. While the agreement does not utilize a purely final-offer arbitration procedure, it does provide a peaceful arbitral terminal point should any issues prove to be unresolvable at the bargaining table.

The agreement provides one bargaining procedure to resolve national issues and another to resolve local issues. On the national level, both sides are to start talks no later than February (they actually started on January 30 in 1974). If an agreement is not reached by April 15, either party can submit unresolved bargaining issues to an impartial arbitration panel, which will have authority to render final and binding decisions.

This arbitration panel will be made up of one

union representative, one representative of the companies, and three impartial arbitrators selected by both sides. At least two of these three arbitrators to be chosen by both sides must be persons thoroughly familiar with collective bargaining agreements in the steel industry. The panel hears any such disputes during May and must render its decisions no later than July 10. The balance of July is to be available for implementation of the panel's award. The Basic Steel agreement was renewed on August 1, 1974.

Will this procedure work in the long run? Well, perhaps the parties themselves are in the best position to answer that—especially the union, since it is the party relinquishing that long-cherished, but outmoded weapon, the strike. I. W. Abel, President of the United Steelworkers of America, has publicly stated:

I am optimistic that the agreement will work. First, the industry and the union have agreed to try this experimental approach on a one-time basis. The parties know that if the experiment fails, there may never be another chance to establish a long period of industrial peace in the industry. We realize that failure this time could lead to a long, disastrous strike three years later. I believe that these realities will be uppermost in the minds of both company and union negotiators as they meet next year. And it will put on all of us a degree of pressure that we may never have felt before—if the parties sincerely seek a long-range stabilized labor-management relationship, and I think we do.

Also, it is only natural for both sides to prefer a settlement shaped by themselves, and not by a third party.

The parties themselves know the problems best and they also know what solutions will work best. A third party dictating the terms of a settlement might not be aware of technical problems that may, unwittingly, stem from an imposed settlement.

The need to formulate contract conditions that are workable and acceptable to both sides will serve as additional pressure to resolve issues independent of the arbitration machinery that has been established. In fact, I predict that chances are reasonably good that an entire agreement on national issues could be negotiated without submitting anything to the arbitration panel. This certainly will be the objective of the union.[97]

One comes away from this reading with the impression that the parties are more intimidated by the contemplation of a third party's deciding things for them than they previously have been by the worry and fear of a strike. Consequently, not only does this new arrangement replace a costly and potentially violent terminal point for bargaining with an inexpensive and peaceful one, but it also motivates the parties to bargain more responsibly and to strive much harder for solutions at the bargaining table. Certainly this arrangement provides every indication that it is among the better ways for labor and management to negotiate contracts.

In a sense the steel agreement was perhaps the long-delayed outgrowth of the traumatic 116-day industrywide steel strike of 1959. Although neither party has yet fully recovered from the consequences of that strike, it may have been a blessing in disguise. It no doubt largely accounts for the absence of any steel strike in the intervening years.

And the parties' mutual reluctance to experience another industrywide strike has led to the very maturity which made this new arrangement possible.

Early-Bird Negotiations

This technique is one which is also being employed by the Steelworkers and the steel industry negotiators. Their labor agreements do not expire until August 1, yet they begin their bargaining talks around February 1. Of course, in that particular situation, they are obliged to do so in order to have their unresolved issues, if any, given to the selected arbitration panel by April 15.

More typically, however, labor agreements call for the contract to be eligible for reopening during the 60 days prior to its expiration. All of these 60 days are seldom used, and usually the parties do not even meet each other for the first time until they are within 45 days or 30 (or even fewer) days of the expiration date. The natural result of this approach is that the parties are already experiencing the pressures of the impending deadline before they even have met.

In recent years an insignificantly few parties have begun chipping away at the issues far earlier than in the past. This early-bird effort serves as a safety valve that helps to relieve some of the pressures that have traditionally surrounded the negotiating table as strike deadlines approach. The Federal Mediation and Conciliation Service has been promoting this early negotiating procedure to minimize strikes. Such precrisis mediation has had some success in bargaining situations with a bad history of strikes.

Where enlightened self-interest has dictated to both parties that they avoid a strike, alternatives to strikes have been accepted by the parties and appear to be working. Recent examples include the steel companies and the Steelworkers' settlement, the Pacific Maritime Association/International Longshoremen's and Warehousemen's Union no-strike effort, the San Francisco newspaper settlement, and the Iowa beef processors' 1973 negotiations.

Granted, the early-bird technique will not guarantee against the possibility of a work stoppage, but it may in some cases reduce the probability. Since it can mean fewer big strikes, what can be the logical objections to it? To those dedicated to the pursuit and attainment of lasting labor peace, there can be no persuasive arguments against any such techniques.

Benefits of Early-Bird Negotiations. Actually, no bona fide bargaining need take place at the outset. More often than not, the parties have only come together *during* the term of the agreement over grievance and arbitration issues. These early meetings can permit an exchange of demands and a thorough review for purposes of familiarization with the respective proposals of each. The following topics can be explored: the financial condition of the employer; wage trends and surveys and current statistics as to price index changes; the history of grievances and the most troublesome and pervasive issues they have raised; and anticipated operational and manpower problems.

It often happens that one or both of the chief negotiators are new, and they therefore are strangers to each other. These early forums can then provide an opportunity in advance of hard bargaining for the spokesmen to get to know one another. Not knowing your bargaining adversary, nor being able to understand or anticipate him, can result in bargaining complications that have nothing to do with the complexity of the issues being discussed. Early discussions can substantially alleviate such misunderstandings. And for those principal spokesmen who, as is common, are from corporate headquarters or the international union office, there is an opportunity to be filled in on the day-to-day workings of the labor agreement.

Where early-bird negotiations are not utilized and agreement is still reached early, the terms of the newly ratified contract are traditionally not put into effect until the old one expires. Under the early-bird approach, however, early agreement and ratification are encouraged, with the understanding that the new contract terms will be put into effect immediately upon membership acceptance.

Mediation-Arbitration

Of the innovative labor-management techniques that have been considered in recent years, mediation-arbitration is perhaps one of the more flexible and creative.

In conventional mediation, the role of the mediator is limited. He appears at a time of crisis but has no power to prevent a strike. He has little time to accomplish more than to fashion short-term, pragmatic results (if successful). His objective is to get the dispute settled quickly and peacefully, with little regard for the substance of the settlement.

In conventional interest arbitration, the role of the arbitrator is also limited. He is remote from the parties and the issue and is bound by formal procedures. In the conventional process, witnesses testify, exhibits are introduced, and a record is kept.

In mediation-arbitration the same individual serves as mediator and, if it becomes necessary, arbitrator. As such he must combine the best qualities of both offices: the conciliatory talents of the mediator with the objectivity and authority of the arbitrator. The dual role enables him to have full insights into the positions of the two parties and to realize what issues are the most essential to each.

In mediation-arbitration no transcripts are kept and therefore no precedents are set by technical procedures or arbitrators' opinions. One of the larger benefits of the process is that it gives the parties a better opportunity to consider the issues reasonably and to create some constructive solutions that will be valid over the long term.

Unfortunately this process is too new and has been used too infrequently to date to permit accurate assessment of its long-term acceptability and viability. However, where it has been used, the reactions consistently have been positive.

A Land of Few Strikes

Before leaving this section, it may be interesting to discuss a lovely and prosperous country in which strike prevention has been quite successful. The unions and employers of Switzerland have almost eliminated the strike as a means of settling labor disputes. In 1960, with a population of 5,429,000 and a total work force of 2,514,000, Switzerland had eight strikes involving 20 firms and 214 employees. The strikes resulted in a total loss of 1,016 working days.[98]

Strikes against public services are banned in Switzerland, as are general strikes during an official mediation procedure. Otherwise, there is no law against strikes in Switzerland. And yet labor peace prevails mainly because the people want it that way.

The labor peace primarily flows from a peace agreement between the Employers' Association of the Swiss Engineering and Metal Industries and the five unions of those industries and was formally signed in 1937. The peace agreement bans all strikes and provides that all issues must be settled peaceably, that is, either through negotiations, mediation, or arbitration. Under its terms, the unions and the Employers' Association each deposited 250,000 francs of "caution money" in the National Bank of Switzerland to guarantee performance under the agreement.

Other industries there have adopted peace pacts modeled after this agreement. These pacts include provisions for conciliation and arbitration similar to those in the metal industry agreement, with certain other provisions adapted to the needs of the particular industry.

CONCLUSION

THE PRESERVATION of the collective bargaining relationship depends in no small part on techniques for an equitable and expeditious resolution of industrial conflict. The strike is an outmoded, useless method of settling industrial disputes. To suggest that we cannot have collective bargaining without reliance directly on the strike as the moving force is the same as saying that in international relations we cannot have diplomacy if we renounce warfare. As David L. Cole has said, precisely the contrary is true in both the labor and international fields.

Collective bargaining has become a method of protecting the old against the new, of retarding technological change, and of protecting a vested interest in obsolete methods.

The structure of labor unions has always been a derivative of the structure of industry, which is largely a product of technology. Between 1948 and 1967, there was a substantial increase in the share of assets controlled by the 200 largest U.S. manufacturing corporations. During the last two years of that period, merger activity reached an all-time high. By 1967, the 100 largest corporations held 47.6 percent of the assets of all manufacturing corporations, or about the same share as held by the 200 largest in 1948. Most of the larger companies are conglomerate enterprises operating on the average in about 11 different industries.

Whether such developments are good or bad is beyond the scope of this work. But they are a fact of life, and labor unions are reacting to them—in the use of computers, coordinated bargaining, mergers, and the like. Certainly in the not-too-distant future will come a merger of labor unions comparable to the industrial mergers, resulting in more multiplant, multi-employer, and industrywide bargaining and in more-coordinated bargaining.

The eventual outcome of that is fearful to contemplate. Like the hapless centipede on the flypaper, whose efforts to release a trapped leg lead to more and more legs' becoming stuck, our efforts to extricate ourselves from this self-imposed dilemma will, if we keep it up, soon have us entirely immobilized.

The role of the United States in its relations with other nations of the world, its programs for assuring adequate economic growth and full employment, the effects of major technological developments on the economy at large, and the functions of wages, prices, and profits in the economic system are all matters of vital interest to the nation and its citizens. The day will come—and it is not so very far off—when the labor-management com-

munity will have to give these matters the consideration they merit, if it is to preserve the free and voluntary nature of collective bargaining in this country.

The strike has too long been regarded as essential to the process of collective bargaining. It takes
very little research to demonstrate that historically
this proposition has been open to question. Over a
century ago, and for more than a generation, major
industries in Great Britain submitted their unsettled disputes over wages and working conditions to
arbitration. Before then, moreover, a similar pattern was followed for years in France and Belgium.

To those who argue that the experiences and
conditions in this country are different, it must be
pointed out that we too have engaged in a good
deal of arbitrating of contract-making disputes. The
printing trade had such programs. Since 1896, the
constitution of the Amalgamated Street Railway
Union has required the union's locals to offer arbitration before calling a strike. Similar practices have
been followed by the IBEW in the public utility
industry, and in milk processing and delivery. Air
transportation companies and the pilots' organizations have become strong advocates of third party
procedures of various kinds in their efforts to keep
service going, and retail establishments and newspapers have resorted to arbitration rather than to
tests of strength. In other words, reliance on the
strike as the vital or essential force in labor negotiations has not always been accepted as an immu-
table tenet.

A false halo has been placed around the collective bargaining process, mainly by legislators and

academicians but also by too many who have participated in labor negotiations. In some circles in this country it has been a sacrilege to suggest that the time has come to look for substitutes for strikes.

In the competitive world market that we now operate in, it is obvious that there are many businesses where neither management nor labor can afford the outmoded luxury of free collective bargaining with strikes or lockouts or even the threat of such economic reprisals.

Unless management, labor, and government join together to find workable alternatives to strikes, the products and prestige of American industry will continue to decline in the world marketplace. Should that decline continue, it would lead to the decline of the United States as the world's foremost economic and political power. And historians of the future would cite as a major contributing factor the fact that collective bargaining, backed by the right to strike, remained to the end a basic government labor policy.

Appendix 1

EXPEDITED ARBITRATION PROCEDURE
General Electric Company and Electrical Workers (IUE)

THE PARTIES agree to instruct the American Arbitration Association to request panel Arbitrators to provide available alternative hearing dates, as soon as possible, so as to provide for a hearing at least within sixty (60) days of the date of their appointment for the hearing of all discharge and upgrading cases between the parties. This instruction is for a trial period running from June 25, 1973 to June 27, 1976.

In order to effectively implement this trial procedure concerning the expedited scheduling of hearings in discharge and upgrading cases, it is expected that the American Arbitration Association will:

(1) Transmit, with appropriate information, a copy of this agreement to each panel arbitrator so that he will be aware of the trial period for the required expedited scheduling of discharge and upgrading cases.

(2) Request from the panel arbitrator, at the time of his appointment, two or three proposed alternative hearing dates for hearing dates within sixty (60) days of his

appointment in all discharge and upgrading cases for the trial period beginning June 25, 1973 to June 27, 1976.

(3) Communicate proposed alternative hearing dates to designated representatives of the parties promptly and secure a firm commitment on a hearing date.

(4) Schedule agreed upon hearing dates in accordance with regular procedure.

By agreement of the parties on July 2, 1973.

TRIAL PROCEDURES FOR ELIMINATION OF WRITTEN OPINIONS AND TRANSCRIPTS

The Company and the Union have hereby agreed to trial procedures to eliminate (I) written opinions and (II) transcripts in certain designated cases. The trial period for the testing of the expedited procedures shall run from June 25, 1973 to June 27, 1976 unless either party gives the other at least one month written notice of its desire to terminate these trial procedures at an earlier date. Thus, any grievances where the agreement to arbitrate arises on and after June 25, 1973 and up to and including June 27, 1976 shall be governed by these expedited and cost-cutting procedures unless earlier terminated.

I. WRITTEN OPINIONS

A. Written Opinions shall not be given by a panel arbitrator in the arbitration of all discipline and discharge grievances, except where the submission to arbitration would require the arbitrator to:

(1) Interpret one or more provisions of the National Agreement; or

(2) Rule on "procedural" questions, such as arbitrability or due process.

B. To implement the criteria set forth in I.A., above, the parties agree to the following procedure:

(1) If the party requesting arbitration believes the grievance meets the criteria, that party would so indicate in its written request for arbitration.

(2) If the party requesting arbitration does not indicate in its written request for arbitration that it believes the case meets the criteria, the other party may indicate that it believes the grievance meets the criteria in its written agreement to arbitrate.

(3) If the party requesting arbitration indicates that it believes the grievance meets the criteria in I.A. in its request for arbitration, or if the other party so indicates in its written agreement to arbitrate, the American Arbitration Association will instruct the designated arbitrator to issue an Award only without an opinion subject to the discretion given the Arbitrator in I.B. (4). Under this Agreement an Award without an Opinion shall consist of a summary statement by the Arbitrator of no more than two pages which briefly sets forth the basis of his Award.

(4) If either party disagrees with the indication of the other party [provided for in I.B. (1) and (2)] that the grievance meets the criteria set forth in I.A. and C. that party may request a written Opinion from the Arbitrator so long as such request is made before the hearing is closed. When such a request is made by either party, the Arbitrator shall rule whether a written Opinion is waived under the criteria set forth in I.A. and C.

(5) If evidence is admitted during the hearing at the instance of either party which, in the judgment of the other party, would change the case from one meeting the criteria in I.A., above, to a case not meeting the criteria, the other party may then demand a written Opinion so long as such demand is made before the oral

hearing is closed—notwithstanding prior agreement to waive the Opinion. This provision, however, should not be interpreted in any way to imply that either party would agree to the introduction of evidence at the hearing which would change the nature of the case.

C. As further guidelines for the parties, the parties agree that the above procedure is not intended to eliminate written opinions with respect to any grievance involving discipline or discharge where the basic issue of the grievance involved the interpretation of the contract or of procedural matters, but only in the arbitration of those grievances, the arbitral determination of which depends essentially upon a resolution of credibility issues. Other disciplinary or discharge grievances such as those which are inextricably intertwined with the construction of a contractual provision or which for example raise an issue of timeliness of the processing of the grievance, due process, or an issue of an allegedly belated expansion of the submission would require an opinion.

II. Transcripts

A. With respect to transcripts, it is the desire of the parties to eliminate the expense and avoid the delay of transcripts in those discharge and discipline grievances where:

(1) The interpretation of one or more provisions of the collective bargaining agreement is not involved; and

(2) There is no "procedural" question such as arbitrability or due process; and

(3) The only issue in a discharge or discipline case is whether the discharge or discipline was imposed for just cause.

B. To implement the criteria set forth in II.A., the parties agree to advise their respective representatives to refrain from requesting transcripts during the trial period for those hearings where the issues presented meet the criteria.

C. As a guideline for the parties, it is the intent to generally eliminate transcripts during the trial period in those cases in which the Company and the Union have agreed to instruct the American Arbitration Association to direct the Arbitrator to issue an Award only without an Opinion. Transcripts may also be eliminated by mutual agreement in other appropriate cases where the parties have agreed upon a specific submission.

By agreement of the parties on July 2, 1973.

Appendix 2

STEEL INDUSTRY ARBITRATION AGREEMENT

THIS EXPERIMENTAL NEGOTIATING AGREEMENT dated March 29, 1973, is between United Steelworkers of America (hereinafter referred to as the "Union") and the Coordinating Committee Steel Companies (hereinafter referred to as the "Companies") and is applicable to Union-represented employees in the plants listed in Appendix A (hereinafter referred to as "employees").

It is highly desirable to provide stability of steel operations, production and employment for the benefit of the employees, customers, suppliers, and stockholders of the Companies, and the public. To attain this objective requires that the Union and the Companies settle issues which arise in collective bargaining in such a way as to avoid industrywide strikes or lockouts or government intervention. The parties are confident that they possess the requisite ability and skills to resolve whatever differences may exist between them in future negotiations through the process of free collective bargaining.

The parties believe that the Agreement will enhance the success of the 1974 negotiations, will avert a strike-hedge steel inventory buildup and will reduce foreign steel imports into the United States.

In view of the foregoing, it is agreed by the Union and the Companies that they will make every effort to resolve through negotiations any differences which may arise in bargaining. After thorough bargaining in good faith the parties may submit any unresolved issue (which is not excluded from arbitration by this Agreement or any subsequent agreement between the parties) to final and binding arbitration by an Impartial Arbitration Panel in accordance with the provisions hereinafter set forth. The submission of any issue to final and binding arbitration shall not preclude the parties from continuing to bargain on such issue prior to the issuance of a decision by the Impartial Arbitration Panel.

A. STRIKES AND LOCKOUTS
Except as otherwise provided in Paragraph 5 of Section D of this Agreement, the Union on behalf of the employees agrees not to engage in strikes, work stoppages or concerted refusals to work in support of its bargaining demands, and the Companies agree not to resort to lockouts of employees to support their bargaining positions.

B. WAGE INCREASES
1. Effective August 1, 1974, the rates in effect July 31, 1974, shall be increased as follows:

a. Each standard hourly job class rate for nonincentive jobs shall be increased by 3% of such rate.

b. Each hourly job class rate for incentive jobs shall be increased by the same cents per hour as the corresponding standard hourly job class rate for nonincentive jobs with no increase in the hourly additive.*

* The adjustment each August 1 for an employee on a job covered by an existing incentive plan not based on the Incentive Calculation Rate Scale shall be made in the same manner as the adjustments that were made effective August 1, 1971.

c. Each standard salary rate shall be increased by 3%.

2. Effective August 1, 1975, the rates established by B-1 above shall be increased as follows:

a. Each standard hourly job class rate for nonincentive jobs shall be increased by 3% of such rate.

b. Each hourly job class rate for incentive jobs shall be increased by the same cents per hour as the corresponding standard hourly job class rate for nonincentive jobs with no increase in the hourly additive.*

c. Each standard salary rate shall be increased by 3%.

3. Effective August 1, 1976, the rates established by B-2 above shall be increased as follows:

a. Each standard hourly job class rate for nonincentive jobs shall be increased by 3% of such rate.

b. Each hourly job class rate for incentive jobs shall be increased by the same cents per hour as the corresponding standard hourly job class rate for nonincentive jobs with no increase in the hourly additive.*

c. Each standard salary rate shall be increased by 3%.

4. For hourly paid employees covered by basic labor agreements containing base rates differing from the scales of rates in Appendix A and Appendix A-1 of the basic labor agreement between United States Steel Corporation and the Union covering production and maintenance employees in the steel plants, and for salaried employees covered by basic labor agreements containing base rates differing from the scale of rates in Appendix A of the basic labor

---

* The adjustment each August 1 for an employee on a job covered by an existing incentive plan not based on the Incentive Calculation Rate Scale shall be made in the same manner as the adjustments that were made effective August 1, 1971.

agreement between United States Steel Corporation and the Union covering salaried employees in such plants, the base rates shall be increased each August 1 by the same percentage as set forth above.

C. Bonus
In consideration of the contribution made by employees to stability of steel operations, each employee as of August 1, 1974, shall receive $150.00 in the pay period next closed and calculated after September 30, 1974. Any dispute as to whether an employee is eligible for a bonus payment will be a proper subject for the grievance and arbitration procedure under the applicable basic labor agreement.

D. The Negotiations and Arbitration
1. It is the intention of the parties hereto that all issues, except as otherwise provided herein, which arise in collective bargaining between the parties shall be either resolved by them or decided by the Impartial Arbitration Panel. In order to achieve this objective:

a. The negotiating teams representing the Union and the Companies will begin negotiations not later than February 1, 1974, for new agreements applicable to employees. If, after the date of this Agreement, a Union-represented bargaining unit becomes covered by a basic labor agreement covering plants listed in Appendix A, because of a provision of such basic labor agreement making it applicable to such unit, such unit shall be added to Appendix A.

b. Not later than April 15, 1974, the parties shall:
(1) reach a full settlement agreement on all issues; or
(2) agree that certain specified issues are settled (through collective bargaining or special proce-

dures) and certain other issues will be submitted to the Impartial Arbitration Panel (established in accordance with the provisions of Section E of this Agreement) for final and binding decision; or (3) withdraw all offers and counter-offers and, except as otherwise provided herein, submit to the Impartial Arbitration Panel for final and binding decision such issues as the parties respectively may urge upon the Panel.

2. If arbitration is required, the parties shall not later than April 20, 1974, submit to the Impartial Arbitration Panel an agreed-upon list of issues to be submitted to the Panel or, if no agreement has been reached on such a list, their respective lists or formulations of such issues. Within twenty days thereafter each party shall submit to the Panel and to each other a detailed written statement supporting its position on the issues before the Panel for determination. Within ten days subsequent to the filing of written statements of position with the Panel, the parties may file with the Panel and exchange written replies to each other's statements, which shall be restricted to responses to the other party's written statement. Subsequent to the receipt of the written statements of position and replies, the Panel shall conduct hearings and shall render its decisions in accordance with Paragraphs 4, 5 and 6 of Section E of this Agreement.

3. Prior to the commencement of hearings by the Panel, representatives of the parties shall meet with the Chairman of the Panel and establish procedures to be followed at the hearings with respect to the following matters: (i) order of presentation, (ii) allocation of time for presentation, (iii) designation of persons to present and comment on parties' positions, and (iv) such other procedural matters as the Chairman and the representatives may agree upon.

4. The Panel's decision shall be rendered not later than midnight, July 10, 1974. Subsequent to the issuance of the Panel's decision, the parties shall have until midnight, July 20, 1974, to reach agreement as to any contract language and any other steps required to implement the Panel's decision. Absent final agreement by the parties by July 20, 1974, as to such language or other implementing steps, either party may immediately refer any such unresolved questions to the Panel which shall make a final and binding determination on such questions on or before midnight, July 31, 1974.

5. Local collective bargaining issues

   a. Definition: A local collective bargaining issue is an issue entered at plant level, proposing establishment of or change in a condition of employment at that particular plant which:

   (1) would not, if adopted, be inconsistent with any provision of a company agreement (as defined below) or involve any addition to or modification of any such provision or agreement;

   (2) would not be an arbitrable grievance as defined in the applicable basic labor agreement; and

   (3) does not relate to a grievance settlement or an arbitration award; provided, however, this subparagraph (3) does not apply to nonarbitrable grievances.

   Subparagraph (2) above shall not exclude an issue which involved a local agreement or practice relying for enforceability on Section 2-B of the basic labor agreements between United States Steel Corporation and the Union and its counterpart provisions in the agreements of the other Companies.

   The term "company agreement" means any basic labor agreement and all related appendices, understandings, or agreements, including those covering pensions, insurance, SUB or SVP, which contain the kinds of provisions, although not in identical language, included in such agreements between the International Union and the United States Steel Corporation. Any provision of any company agreement that is solely applicable to a particular plant and is not the kind of provision contained in such agreements between the International Union and the United States Steel Corporation shall not be considered part of a company agreement for the purpose of this definition.

    b. Procedure for disposition: The parties shall make every effort to settle local collective bargaining issues and in order to achieve this objective shall proceed as follows:

    (1) Discussions with respect to these issues shall commence at plant level at such time as the parties locally shall deem necessary but in no event later than April 1, 1974. This date shall likewise be the cutoff date and no additional issues, except for those issues which thereafter arise as a result of changed conditions, may subsequently be initiated by either party under the procedures of this Agreement at plant level.

    (2) Any local issue not disposed of by May 1, 1974, shall be referred to and dealt with by the respective Chairman of the Union-Company negotiating committee.

    (3) Should any such issue or issues initiated by the Union remain unresolved as of June 10, 1974, the Union Co-Chairman shall decide whether the issue or issues shall be withdrawn or put to a secret ballot vote available to all employees at that plant as defined in Appendix A, who worked or were on vacation in the last pay period closed on or before June 10, 1974. Such election, to be valid, must take place no later than June 30, 1974.

Every such eligible employee shall be entitled to a ballot furnished by the International Union and appropriate ballot boxes, properly supervised, will be made available for the casting of such ballots. Such ballots shall be collected and counted by tellers selected in conformance with International Union procedures. If a majority of those voting vote in favor of a strike, and if the matter is not otherwise resolved, the matter shall no later than July 8, 1974, be referred by the Union Co-Chairman to the President of the International Union along with a request for permission to strike the plant in which the issue or issues originated. His decision on the request for permission to strike shall be forwarded in writing to the Union Co-Chairman with a copy to the Company Co-Chairman not later than July 15, 1974. Should permission to strike be granted by the President of the International Union, he shall at the same time specify the date on which the strike, if it is to occur, must commence, which shall not be earlier than the first scheduled turn of August 1, 1974, and such strike shall be confined to the plant where the issue or issues originated and as defined in Appendix A. The right to strike pursuant to permission granted by the President of the International Union shall automatically be canceled and the issue between the parties deemed resolved if the strike does not commence on the first scheduled turn of the date specified by the President of the International Union except as the parties at the International-Company level shall agree to another date.

Should any local collective bargaining issue or issues initiated by a Company remain unresolved as of June 10, 1974, the Company shall decide whether the issue or issues shall be withdrawn or become the basis for a lockout at the plant involved. The requirements as to timetable and date of commencement of any lockout by any Company shall be the same as those set out above for strikes over local collective bargaining issues, as more specifically set forth in the balance of this paragraph. The Company's decision shall be forwarded in writing to the Union Co-Chairman not later than July 15, 1974. Should the Company decide to lock out at a plant in support of a local collective bargaining issue or issues, the notice shall specify the date on which the lockout, if it is to occur, must commence, which shall not be earlier than the first scheduled turn of August 1, 1974, and such lockout shall be confined to the plant where the issue or issues originated and as defined in Appendix A. The right to lock out shall automatically be canceled and the issue between the parties deemed resolved if the lockout does not commence on the first scheduled turn of the date specified in the notice except as the parties at the International-Company level shall agree to another date.

Any such strike or lockout shall cease upon the resolution of the local collective bargaining issue or issues because of which such strike or lockout commenced.

6. Issues excluded from arbitration. The Impartial Arbitration Panel shall not have jurisdiction of, and the parties shall not present to the Panel, any issue affecting or relating to:

a. The Section 2-B Local Working Conditions provisions of the basic labor agreements between the United States Steel Corporation and the Union and counterpart provisions in the agreements of the other Companies.

b. The Union Membership and Checkoff provisions of any such agreements.

c. The Cost-of-Living Adjustment provisions of any such agreements, but the Panel shall consider the cost of such item in rendering its decisions on wages and other issues presented to it.

d. The uniformity (or current relationship of parity, in the event that uniformity does not prevail) of wages and benefits between and among the various units, plants or operations covered by this Agreement. Nor shall the Panel make any determination which would result in a different application, than has historically prevailed, of the wage or benefit features of its award as among such units, plants or operations.

e. The wage increases and bonus granted under Sections B and C of this Agreement, but the Panel shall consider the cost of such items in rendering its decision on wages and other issues presented to it.

f. The no-strike and no-lockout provisions of any such agreements.

g. The management rights provisions of any such agreements.

E. THE IMPARTIAL ARBITRATION PANEL

1. Appointment. The Impartial Arbitration Panel shall consist of five members, one appointed by the Union, one appointed by the Companies and three impartial members appointed by agreement of the parties. Two of the three impartial members shall be persons who are thoroughly familiar with collective bargaining agreements in the steel industry. The Union and the Companies will inform each other as to the identity of their

respective members on or before February 1, 1974, and also on or before such date agree upon the three impartial members of the Panel and designate a Chairman.

2. Successorship. In the event of refusal to serve, death, incapacity or resignation of any member of the Panel, a successor having essentially the same qualifications as his predecessor on the Panel shall be immediately appointed to fill such vacancy in the manner provided for in the appointment of members in E-1 above.

3. Method of voting. All matters presented to the Panel for its determination shall be decided by a majority vote of the impartial members of the Panel. The members representing the Union and the Companies shall not have a vote. The Panel, prior to a vote on any issue in dispute before it, shall, upon the joint request of the Union's and Companies' members of the Panel, refer the issue back to the parties for further negotiations, provided that such a request is made not later than June 30, 1974.

4. Time and place of hearing. The Panel shall hold hearings at such times and places as agreed to by the parties for the purpose of developing those facts and additional arguments which the parties may desire to present or which the Panel may require. Each of the parties may invite to such hearings such members, employees, representatives and staff as each may desire, who shall be provided with proper identification. The hearings shall begin not later than June 1, 1974.

5. Conduct of the hearing.

   a. The record of the hearings shall include all documents, written statements and exhibits which may be submitted, together with a stenographic record. The Panel shall, in the absence of agreement of the parties, have authority to make whatever reasonable rules are necessary for the conduct of an orderly hearing. In the formulation of such rules the Panel shall be guided by the need to gather full information on all issues in an expeditious, orderly and informal manner. The impartial members of the Panel shall have the authority to limit the number of witnesses which the parties may call in support of their respective positions on any issue before the Panel, when, in their judgment it is necessary to the expeditious inquiry into the dispute.

b. The Panel or any of its members may, at the hearing, call as witnesses such members, employees and representatives of the parties as may be necessary, and may participate in the examination of witnesses for the purpose of expediting the hearings or eliciting material facts. They may also request the parties to produce any evidence which they deem relevant to the issue before them.

c. The hearings may be conducted informally. The receipt of evidence at the hearing need not be governed by statutory or common law rules of evidence.

d. In order to encourage frank discussions between the parties during negotiations, those conversations which occurred and proposals made during such negotiations shall not be referred to in connection with the presentation of any issue to the Panel, except as the parties agree otherwise.

6. Decisions of the Panel

a. All decisions of the Panel shall be in writing and shall set forth the facts and reasons for the Panel's conclusions with sufficient specificity to enable the parties to understand and implement the Panel's decisions.

b. Decisions of the Panel shall be effective as of August 1, 1974, and specific provisions of the award shall become applicable as of dates provided in the award.

c. Decisions of the Panel shall be final and binding on the parties.

7. Duration of the Panel. The members of the Panel shall continue to serve until August 1, 1974, to assist the parties in the interpretation and implementation of the Panel's decisions.

8. Compensation and costs of the Panel. The Union's member of the Panel shall be paid by the Union and the Companies' member of the Panel shall be paid by the Companies. The compensation and expenses of the impartial members of the Panel, as well as the costs incurred by the Panel in conducting the hearings, shall be borne equally by the Union and the Companies.

F. TERM OF THE NEW AGREEMENTS

The term of the new agreements shall be three years.

G. CONTINUATION OF EXISTING AGREEMENT TERMS

Except as contained in or required by the award of the Panel or as agreed to by the parties, the provisions of the existing agreements (except for the Annual Cost-of-Living Adjustment Guarantees Section [Marginal Paragraphs 9.88, 9.89 and the last portion of 9.87, commencing with the word "subject," of the Agreement between the International Union and the United States Steel Corporation] which will no longer be applicable) will be carried forward in the new agreements. Should it become desirable to revise the cost-of-living formula (Marginal Paragraph 9.84 of the Agreement above and counterpart paragraphs of the agreements of the other Companies), the parties will negotiate in an attempt to reach agreement on such revision and, failing such agreement, either party may submit the issue of such revision to arbitration.

H. Term of Experimental Negotiating Agreement
This Agreement shall become effective upon execution
by the officers of the International Union and an authorized official of each of the Companies and shall terminate August 1, 1974, except to the extent that its continuation beyond that date is deemed necessary by the
parties to achieve the objectives of this Agreement.

*United Steelworkers
of America*

*Allegheny Ludlum Industries,
Inc.
Armco Steel Corporation
Bethlehem Steel Corporation
Inland Steel Company
Jones & Laughlin Steel
Corporation
National Steel Corporation
Republic Steel Corporation
United States Steel Corporation
Wheeling-Pittsburgh Steel
Corporation
Youngstown Sheet & Tube
Company*

Appendix 3

SUITS BY AND AGAINST LABOR ORGANIZATIONS
Labor Management Relations Act

Section 301

(a) Suits for violation of contracts between an employer and a labor organization representing employees in an industry affecting commerce as defined in this Act, or between any such labor organizations, may be brought in any district court of the United States having jurisdiction of the parties, without respect to the amount in controversy or without regard to the citizenship of the parties.

(b) Any labor organization which represents employees in an industry affecting commerce as defined in this Act and any employer whose activities affect commerce as defined in this Act shall be bound by the acts of its agents. Any such labor organization may sue or be sued as an entity and in behalf of the employees whom it represents in the courts of the United States. Any money judgment against a labor organization in a district court of the United States shall be enforceable only against the organization as an entity and against its assets, and shall not be enforceable against any individual member or his assets.

(c) For the purposes of actions and proceedings by or against labor organizations in the district courts of the United States, district courts shall be deemed to have jurisdiction of a labor organization (1) in the district in which such organization maintains its principal office, or (2) in any district in which its duly authorized officers or agents are engaged in representing or acting for employee members.

(d) The service of summons, subpoena, or other legal process of any court of the United States upon an officer or agent of a labor organization, in his capacity as such, shall constitute service upon the labor organization.

(e) For the purposes of this section, in determining whether any person is acting as an "agent" of another person so as to make such other person responsible for his acts, the question of whether the specific acts performed were actually authorized or subsequently ratified shall not be controlling.

The above Section has been expanded by the federal courts to cover breach of contract and damage suits, and suits for equitable relief in the form of specific performance of contracts and agreements to arbitrate. [W.E.B.]

Appendix 4

UNFAIR LABOR PRACTICES
Sections 8(b), (c), and (d) of the LMRA

(b) It shall be an unfair labor practice for a labor organization or its agents—

(1) to restrain or coerce (A) employees in the exercise of the rights guaranteed in section 7: Provided, That this paragraph shall not impair the right of a labor organization to prescribe its own rules with respect to the acquisition or retention of membership therein; or (B) an employer in the selection of his representatives for the purposes of collective bargaining or the adjustment of grievances;

(2) to cause or attempt to cause an employer to discriminate against an employee in violation of subsection (a) (3) or to discriminate against an employee with respect to whom membership in such organization has been denied or terminated on some ground other than his failure to tender the periodic dues and the initiation fees uniformly required as a condition of acquiring or retaining membership;

(3) to refuse to bargain collectively with an employer, provided it is the representative of his employees subject to the provisions of section 9(a);

(4) to engage in, or to induce or encourage the employees of any employer to engage in, a strike or a concerted refusal in the course of their employment to use, manufacture, process, transport, or otherwise handle or work on any goods, articles, materials, or commodities or to perform any services, or to threaten, coerce, or restrain any person engaged in commerce or in an industry affecting commerce, where in either case an object thereof is: (A) forcing or requiring any employer or self-employed person to join any labor or employer organization; (B) forcing or requiring any person to cease using, selling, handling, transporting, or otherwise dealing in the products of any other producer, processor, or manufacturer, or to cease doing business with any other person, or forcing or requiring any other employer to recognize or bargain with a labor organization as the representative of his employees unless such labor organization has been certified as the representative of such employees under the provisions of section 9: Provided, That nothing contained in this clause (B) shall be construed to make unlawful, where not otherwise unlawful, any primary strike or primary picketing; (C) forcing or requiring any employer to recognize or bargain with a particular labor organization as the representative of his employees if another labor organization has been certified as the representative of such employees under the provisions of section 9; (D) forcing or requiring any employer to assign particular work to employees in a particular labor organization or in a particular trade, craft, or class rather than to employees in another labor organization or in another trade, craft, or class, unless

such employer is failing to conform to an order or certification of the Board determining the bargaining representative for employees performing such work: Provided, That nothing contained in this subsection (b) shall be construed to make unlawful a refusal by any person to enter upon the premises of any employer (other than his own employer), if the employees of such employer are engaged in a strike ratified or approved by a representative of such employees whom such employer is required to recognize under this Act; Provided, further, That for the purposes of this paragraph (4) only, nothing contained in such paragraph shall be construed to prohibit publicity, other than picketing, for the purpose of truthfully advising the public, including consumers and members of a labor organization, that a product or products are produced by an employer with whom the labor organization has a primary dispute and are distributed by another employer, as long as such publicity does not have an effect of inducing any individual employed by any person other than the primary employer in the course of his employment to refuse to pick up, deliver, or transport any goods, or not to perform any services, at the establishment of the employer engaged in such distribution;

(5) to require of employees covered by an agreement authorized under subsection (a)(3) the payment, as a condition precedent to becoming a member of such organization, of a fee in an amount which the Board finds excessive or discriminatory under all the circumstances. In making such a finding, the Board shall consider, among other relevant factors, the practices and customs of labor organizations in the particular industry, and the wages currently paid to the employees affected; and

(6) to cause or attempt to cause an employer to pay or deliver or agree to pay or deliver any money or other

thing of value in the nature of an exaction, for services which are not performed or not to be performed;

(7) to picket or cause to be picketed, or threaten to picket or cause to be picketed, any employer where an object thereof is forcing or requiring an employer to recognize or bargain with a labor organization as the representative of his employees, or forcing or requiring employees of an employer to accept or select such labor organization as their collective bargaining representative, unless such labor organization is currently certified as the representative of such employees; (A) where the employer has lawfully recognized in accordance with this Act any other labor organization and a question concerning representation may not appropriately be raised under section 9(c) of this Act, (B) where within the preceding twelve months a valid election under section 9(c) of this Act has been conducted, or (C) where such picketing has been conducted without a petition under section 9(c) being filed within a reasonable period of time not to exceed thirty days from the commencement of such picketing: Provided, That when such a petition has been filed the Board shall forthwith, without regard to the provisions of section 9(c)(1) or the absence of a showing of a substantial interest on the part of the labor organization, direct an election in such unit as the Board finds to be appropriate and shall certify the results thereof: Provided further, That nothing in this subparagraph (C) shall be construed to prohibit any picketing or other publicity for the purpose of truthfully advising the public (including consumers) that an employer does not employ members of, or have a contract with, a labor organization, unless an effect of such picketing is to induce any individual employed by any other person in the course of his employment, not to pick up,

deliver or transport any goods or not to perform any services.

Nothing in this paragraph (7) shall be construed to permit any act which would otherwise be an unfair labor practice under this section (8)(b).

(c) The expressing of any views, argument, or opinion, or the dissemination thereof, whether in written, printed, graphic, or visual form, shall not constitute or be evidence of an unfair labor practice under any of the provisions of this Act, if such expression contains no threat of reprisal or force or promise of benefit.

(d) For the purposes of this section, to bargain collectively is the performance of the mutual obligation of the employer and the representative of the employees to meet at reasonable times and confer in good faith with respect to wages, hours, and other terms and conditions of employment, or the negotiation of an agreement, or any question arising thereunder, and the execution of a written contract incorporating any agreement reached if requested by either party, but such obligation does not compel either party to agree to a proposal or require the making of a concession: Provided, That where there is in effect a collective-bargaining contract covering employees in an industry affecting commerce, the duty to bargain collectively shall also mean that no party to such contract shall terminate or modify such contract, unless the party desiring such termination or modification—

(1) serves a written notice upon the other party to the contract of the proposed termination or modification sixty days prior to the expiration date thereof, or in the event such contract contains no expiration date, sixty days prior to the time it is proposed to make such termination or modification;

(2) offers to meet and confer with the other party for the purpose of negotiating a new contract or a contract containing the proposed modifications;

(3) notifies the Federal Mediation and Conciliation Service within thirty days after such notice of the existence of a dispute, and simultaneously therewith notifies that State or Territorial agency established to mediate and conciliate disputes within the State or Territory where the dispute occurred, provided no agreement has been reached by that time; and

(4) continues in full force and effect, without resorting to strike or lockout, all the terms and conditions of the existing contract for a period of sixty days after such notice is given or until the expiration date of such contract, whichever occurs later.

The duties imposed upon employers, employees, and labor organizations by paragraphs (2), (3) and (4) shall become inapplicable upon an intervening certification of the Board, under which the labor organization or individual, which is a party to the contract, has been superseded as or ceased to be the representative of the employees subject to the provisions of section 9(a), and the duties so imposed shall not be construed as requiring either party to discuss or agree to any modification of the terms and conditions contained in a contract for a fixed period, if such modification is to become effective before such terms and conditions can be reopened under the provisions of the contract. Any employee who engages in a strike within the sixty-day period specified in this subsection shall lose his status as an employee of the employer engaged in the particular labor dispute, for the purposes of sections 8, 9 and 10 of this Act, as amended, but such loss of status for such employee shall terminate if and when he is reemployed by such employer.

Thus it can be seen that while a strike (even one where there is a no-strike clause) may not seem to be an unfair labor practice on its face, if it can be linked with a refusal to bargain, or a secondary boycott attempt, or compelling recognition while another union is certified or while a contract bar exists, or a jurisdictional dispute, or attempt by the union through strike violence to deny employees their right not to participate in the strike, or unlawful denial of union membership, or "make work," or extortion, or recognition picketing without a representative election petition being timely filed, recourse may be had to the NLRB. Sometimes, the mere filing of a charge has desirable results in that it unsettles the union, gives the employer a tactical bargaining weapon, and may give the union officials an excuse to go to their membership with dignity and request a wavering strike be called off. Furthermore, if it can be shown that the objective or means of a strike were unlawful, the strikers are removed from the protection of Taft-Hartley and the NLRB.

Appendix 5

AMERICAN ARBITRATION ASSOCIATION
*Rules for Expedited Arbitration**

1. Agreement of Parties—These Rules shall apply whenever the parties have agreed to arbitrate under them, in the form obtaining at the time the arbitration is initiated.

2. Appointment of Neutral Arbitrator—The AAA shall appoint a single neutral arbitrator from its Panel of Labor Arbitrators, who shall hear and determine the case promptly.

3. Initiation of Expedited Arbitration Proceeding—Cases may be initiated by joint submission in writing, or in accordance with a collective bargaining agreement.

4. Qualifications of Neutral Arbitrator—No person shall serve as a neutral Arbitrator in any arbitration in which that person has any financial or personal interest in the result of the arbitration. Prior to accepting an appointment, the prospective Arbitrator shall disclose any circumstances likely to prevent a prompt hearing or to create a presumption of bias. Upon receipt of such in-

* Reprinted by permission of the American Arbitration Association.

formation, the AAA shall immediately replace that Arbitrator or communicate the information to the parties.

5. Vacancy—The AAA is authorized to substitute another Arbitrator if a vacancy occurs or if an appointed Arbitrator is unable to serve promptly.

6. Time and Place of Hearing—The AAA shall fix a mutually convenient time and place of the hearing, notice of which must be given at least 24 hours in advance. Such notice may be given orally.

7. Representation by Counsel—Any party may be represented at the hearing by counsel or other representative.

8. Attendance at Hearings—Persons having a direct interest in the arbitration are entitled to attend hearings. The Arbitrator may require the retirement of any witness during the testimony of other witnesses. The Arbitrator shall determine whether any other person may attend the hearing.

9. Adjournments—Hearings shall be adjourned by the Arbitrator only for good cause, and an appropriate fee will be charged by the AAA against the party causing the adjournment.

10. Oaths—Before proceeding with the first hearing, the Arbitrator shall take an oath of office. The Arbitrator may require witnesses to testify under oath.

11. No Stenographic Record—There shall be no stenographic record of the proceedings.

12. Proceedings—The hearing shall be conducted by the Arbitrator in whatever manner will most expeditiously permit full presentation of the evidence and the arguments of the parties. The Arbitrator shall make an appropriate minute of the proceedings. Normally, the hearing shall be completed within one day. In unusual circumstances, and for good cause shown, the Arbitrator may schedule an additional hearing, within five days.

13. Arbitration in the Absence of a Party—The arbi-

tration may proceed in the absence of any party who, after due notice, fails to be present. An award shall not be made solely on the default of a party. The Arbitrator shall require the attending party to submit supporting evidence.

14. Evidence—The Arbitrator shall be the sole judge of the relevancy and materiality of the evidence offered.

15. Evidence by Affidavit and Filing of Documents—The Arbitrator may receive and consider evidence in the form of an affidavit, but shall give appropriate weight to any objections made. All documents to be considered by the Arbitrator shall be filed at the hearing. There shall be no posthearing briefs.

16. Close of Hearings—The Arbitrator shall ask whether parties have any further proofs to offer or witnesses to be heard. Upon receiving negative replies, the Arbitrator shall declare and note the hearing closed.

17. Waiver of Rules—Any party who proceeds with the arbitration after knowledge that any provisions or requirement of these Rules has not been complied with and who fails to state his objections thereto in writing shall be deemed to have waived his right to object.

18. Servicing of Notices—Any papers or process necessary or proper for the initiation or continuation of an arbitration under these Rules and for any court action in connection therewith or for the entry of judgment on an Award made thereunder, may be served upon such party (a) by mail addressed to such party or its attorney at its known address, or (b) by personal service, or (c) as otherwise provided in these Rules.

19. Time of Award—The award shall be rendered promptly by the Arbitrator and, unless otherwise agreed by the parties, not later than five business days from the date of the closing of the hearing.

20. Form of Award—The Award shall be in writing

and shall be signed by the Arbitrator. If the Arbitrator determines that an opinion is necessary, it shall be in summary form.

21. Delivery of Award to Parties—Parties shall accept as legal delivery of the award the placing of the award or a true copy thereof in the mail by the AAA, addressed to such party at its last known address or to its attorney, or personal service of the award, or the filing of the award in any manner which may be prescribed by law.

22. Expenses—The expenses of witnesses for either side shall be paid by the party producing such witnesses.

23. Interpretation and Application of Rules—The Arbitrator shall interpret and apply these Rules insofar as they relate to his powers and duties. All other Rules shall be interpreted and applied by the AAA, as Administrator.

The AAA has made special arrangements to reduce the cost of arbitration under these rules. Details are available at the AAA regional office administering the case.

Appendix 6

STRIKE WORK AGREEMENT

THIS STRIKE WORK AGREEMENT, made and entered into on the 20th day of May, 1964, has been amended as of this 17th day of June, 1965, by and between the Dunbar Furniture Corporation of Indiana, Berne, Indiana, its successors or assigns, hereinafter called the company

and

the Upholsterers' International Union of North America affiliated with the AFL-CIO, hereinafter designated as the Union, acting through its agency, Upholsterers' Furniture and Wood Workers' Local Union No. 222, and under charter from the said Union, for itself and in behalf of the employees now employed and hereinafter employed by the company and collectively designated herein as the employees, hereinafter called the union.

Labor Agreement

The company and the union have a Collective Bargaining Agreement and it is agreed that this Strike Work Agreement and the attached Fiduciary Agreement are subsidiary agreements to the Collective Bargaining Agreement.

I. PROCEDURE

A. *Notice*

In case the union decides to strike or the company decides to have a lockout after a collective bargaining agreement expires it is agreed that the Strike Work procedure as outlined in the agreement will be in effect.

The union will send written notice of the decision to strike to the company or the company will send official written notice of the lockout to the local union.

Starting with the first payroll week after the notice is received the Strike Work procedure will be in effect as outlined in this agreement.

The collective bargaining agreement is reinstated and will continue in force for the entire Strike Work period.

B. *Work Deductions*

There will be no stoppage of work.

All employees will continue to work during the Strike Work period.

One-third of the earnings of all employees in the unit will be withheld and placed in the Strike Work Trust Fund in the custody of the Bank named in the Fiduciary Agreement.

The company will place in the fund each week an amount of money equal to the total amount paid by all employees that week.

C. *Periods—Refunds*

1. First period—four weeks—all money returned.

If the Strike Work is settled inside of four weeks, all of the money will be returned to the employees and the company. The bank will donate its services.

2. Second period—two weeks—75% returned.

If the Strike Work is settled in the next two weeks, 75% of the money paid will be returned to the employees and the company, less 10¢ per check issued in the distribution process.

3. Third period—one week—50% returned.

If the Strike Work is settled in the next one week, 50% of the money will be returned to the employees and the company, less 10¢ per check issued in the distribution process.

4. Fourth period—one week—25% returned.

If the Strike Work is settled in the next one week, 25% of the money will be returned to the employees and the company, less 10¢ per check issued in the distribution process.

II. OLD-FASHIONED STRIKE OR LOCKOUT

If the Strike Work has not been settled by the end of the fourth period (8th week) then no money will be refunded.

The Strike Work Agreement and the Collective Bargaining Agreement may then be terminated and also there may be an old-fashioned strike or lockout by written notice of either party to the other.

III. AGREEMENT RENEWED

If no such notice has been received by either party at the end of the 9th week after the Strike Work started then the last agreement will be automatically renewed, without change for one year. The expiration date will then be one year from the written date of expiration in the last written agreement.

IV. ARBITRATION

Any unresolved dispute among the parties as to the meaning or application of this agreement or any charge by one party against another that the agreement has been violated, shall, by the complaining party, be referred to arbitration under the rules of the American Arbitration Association then pertaining. The arbitrator shall have full authority to remedy any violation or breach of this agreement. The decision of the arbitrator shall be final and binding on all parties. Each party to the arbitration shall bear its own costs and shall equally share the costs of the arbitration. This paragraph shall be applicable, the termination of this agreement or any statute of limitations notwithstanding.

V. RULES

The following rules will be in effect with the start of the first payroll week of a strike or lockout under this Strike Work Agreement.

A. *Retirees*

In case an employee is eligible to retire and does retire, then the money that he has paid into the fund will be refunded to him when he retires. Written proof and authorization will be given to the Fiduciary in a jointly signed statement.

B. *Sick or Injured*

If an employee is sick or injured and received benefits under the UIU Health and Welfare Fund or Workmen's Compensation or other statutory industrial compensation funds, the benefits so received will not be considered as wages.

The money that he has paid into the fund will remain there pending his return.

In case it is proved that he is totally disabled, then any money that he has paid into the Fund will be returned to him immediately. The Fiduciary will be given proof and authorization outlined in A above.

When an employee that has been sick or injured returned to work, then he will receive a refund or will pay additional money so that he will pay the same percent of his wages as other employees. The payments, if any, can be divided into four weekly installments.

C. *Quits*

In case an employee quits or is discharged during the time a Strike Work is going on, he will forfeit and lose all claim to any money that he has paid into the fund. If he should be rehired, he will start as a new employee without seniority.

If the amount that he had paid into the fund was a smaller percent of his weekly wage than others paid, he will pay the difference, before starting to work, to the company and the company will deposit the money so received in the fund.

D. *No Strike or Slow Down*

It is agreed that there will be no strike stoppage or slow down or restrictions of output during the time that the Strike Work is in effect.

In case any such action should occur the company may at its option discipline or discharge any or all of the people taking part in a strike, stoppage, slow down or restriction of output.

In case such action by the company is taken to arbitration to sustain its action it shall only be necessary for the company to prove that the employees so dealt with did actually take part in the above strike, stoppage, slow down or restriction of output.

E. *No Law Suit*

It is agreed that the International Union or the Local Union or any of its agents or officers, or any employees will not bring any legal action against the company or the fiduciary. The company will not bring legal action against the International or Local Union or any of their officers or members or against the fiduciary.

F. *No Contributions*

1. During the Strike Work period it is agreed that the International Union and its affiliates shall not directly or indirectly render financial assistance to any of the employees in the bargaining unit.

2. The company agrees that it will not solicit or accept any contributions from any association or from any other source.

3. The employees agree that they will not solicit or accept any contributions or help from local merchants or any other source.

If it is discovered that this section has been violated the guilty party shall pay double the amount received into the trust fund.

VI. DURATION

The Strike Work Agreement may be amended, changed or abolished by mutual agreement between the company and the union.

In witness whereof the parties hereunto set their hands and seals as hereinafter stated, on this 17th day of June, 1965.

Fiduciary Agreement

This Fiduciary Agreement is made and entered into on this the 20th day of May, 1964, by and between the Dunbar Furniture Corporation of Indiana, Berne, Indiana, its successors or assigns, hereinafter called the company,

and the

Upholsterers' International Union of North America affiliated with the AFL-CIO, hereinafter designated as the Union, acting through its agency, Upholsterers' Furniture and Wood Workers' Local Union No. 222, and under charter from the said Union, for itself and in behalf of the employees now employed and hereinafter employed by the company and collectively designated herein as the employees, hereinafter referred to as the union,

with the

First Bank of Berne of Berne, Indiana.

I. Agreements

The company and the union have a collective bargaining agreement.

It is agreed that this Fiduciary Agreement like the Strike Work Agreement is a part of the Collective Bargaining Agreement as of the date that the Strike Work Agreement is signed.

II. The Bank

The company and the union hereby appoint the First Bank of Berne, Berne, Indiana, as the Fiduciary.

The money held in trust by the Fiduciary will be entitled the Strike Work Trust Fund.

III. Trustees

The company and the union will each name a trustee, whose duties are outlined in the agreement. Official written notice of the names of the trustees will be exchanged by the company and the union.

IV. Trust Fund

The Fiduciary will accept and hold the monies and disburse them as outlined.

V. Deduction Procedure

Starting with the first payroll week that a Strike Work as outlined in the attached agreement is in effect the company will withhold one half of the wages of the employees each week that the Strike Work is in effect. For this purpose holiday pay and vacation pay will be considered as wages.

The company will deposit this, together with a company payment of an amount equal to the grand total of the employees' money paid each week that the Strike Work is in effect.

The following procedure will be used:

1. The company will make a list in triplicate show-

ing the name of each employee and the amount of money withheld from each and the grand total and the equal amount that the company pays.

2. The two trust officers will be given a day to inspect and check the lists and on the next business day the checks will be sent by the company to the Fiduciary together with the original list as noted above.

3. One copy of the above list will be retained by the company and one copy will be posted on a bulletin board by the company.

4. With the second payday of the Strike Work the above procedure will be repeated but there will be an additional column showing the total to date deduction from each employee and the total amount paid by the company.

5. When the second list is posted on a bulletin board the first list will be taken down and given to the president of the Local Union for the Union's records.

VI. MONEY RETURNED

In case the Strike Work is settled and money is being returned the following procedure will be used:

1. The company will make a list of employees in the unit, the refund due to each as is provided in the Strike Work Agreement, and the refund due to the company.

2. The trust officer for the union will have as much time as he needs but not to exceed three days to check over this list.

3. Then the trust officer for the union and the company will sign a statement authorizing the fiduciary to send a check for the total gross amount for the employee and a check for the refund due to the company.

4. The company will then issue the checks due to each employee less any deductions required by law or the labor agreement.

5. The company will promptly distribute the checks in the same manner as weekly payroll checks are distributed.

VII. MONEY IN THE FUND

In case any money remains in the fund it can never be used for the benefit of the company or the employees or the union.

(It may be donated to a project or to projects for the general good of citizens of Berne and vicinity.)

VIII. DONATIONS

Either the trust officer for the union or for the company may suggest in writing to the other a project and the proposed amount to be donated.

If the two agree on the amount and the project, then the trust officer for the union will seek approval of the union local and the trust officer for the company will seek approval of the president of the company.

IX. APPROVAL DENIED

If either a trust officer or the local or the company deny approval the bank will be notified by a letter jointly signed by the two trust officers. This matter of approval is not subject to arbitration.

The same procedure will be followed in case this happens a second and third time.

X. TOTAL DONATION

In case there have been two denials as noted above, then by agreement between the company and the local union, the entire fund may be donated to the Berne Ministerial Association to be used as they decide for the general good of the people of Berne and vicinity.

XI. BERNE MINISTERIAL ASSOCIATION

In case there is a third denial, it is agreed that the entire fund will be automatically donated to the Berne Ministerial Association to be used as they decide for the general good of the people of Berne and vicinity.

XII. Dispute

In case there is a dispute as to whether or not there have been three cases where approval was denied then either party may take the case to arbitration.

The arbitrator will only decide the above question and will not alter the agreement or make any suggestions.

The arbitration will be held under the procedure outlined in the collective bargaining agreement. The expense will be borne equally by the company and the union.

XIII. Approval Granted

In case both the company and the local membership approve of the recommendations of the trust officers, then the trust officers will each send to the bank proof of the authorization.

With the above proof they will send jointly signed authorization to the Fiduciary to pay the specified amount to the project or organization named.

XIV. Duration

This *Fiduciary Agreement* is part of the *Strike Work Agreement* and it will remain in effect during the life of the *Strike Work Agreement*.

In witness whereof the parties hereunto set their hands and seals as hereinafter stated, on this 17th day of June, 1965.

REFERENCES

1. Robben W. Fleming, "Arbitration of Contract Issues," Bureau of National Affairs Bulletin 730 (May 24, 1973).
2. Eric F. Jensen, "The Challenges of the 70's," *Seminar on Collective Bargaining* (New York: Niagara University Press, 1972), p. 32.
3. Bureau of National Affairs Bulletin 746 (1971), 1–7.
4. Arthur M. Ross and Paul T. Hartman, *Changing Patterns of Industrial Conflict* (New York: Wiley, 1970).
5. Peter Henle, "Some Reflections on Organized Labor and the New Militants," *Monthly Labor Review*, July, 1969.
6. Frederick Meyers, *The Law and the Strike* (Berkeley: University of California, 1961).
7. "Trouble Plagues the House of Labor," *Business Week*, October, 1972.
8. Bureau of Labor Statistics Report 348 (1970) and BLS Report 1727 (1972).
9. 71 Gerr RF 401–419.
10. "Labor Union and Employee Association Membership, 1970," U.S. Department of Labor press release, September 13, 1971.
11. "Trouble Plagues the House of Labor," *Business Week*, October, 1972.
12. H. G. Laurs, *Unionism and Relative Wages in the United States* (Chicago: University of Chicago Press, 1963), p. 193.
13. Jack Stieber, *A New Approach to Strikes in Public Employment* (Honolulu: University of Hawaii, 1968).

14. McGrady, *Arbitration Journal* 2 (1938), p. 339.
15. Ibid., p. 343.
16. *Contract Clause Finder Collective Bargaining Negotiations and Contracts* (Washington: Bureau of National Affairs, 1970).
17. *Mathis* v. *Panhandle Pipe Line Co.*, 23 LA570 (1954).
18. N. Frieden and A. Ulman, "Arbitration and the War Labor Board," *Harvard Law Review* 309 (1945).
19. Robert Coulson, "Labor Arbitration: The Insecure Profession," Proceedings of NYLB Twentieth Annual Conference on Labor (1967).
20. Bureau of National Affairs Bulletin, 1948 to present.
21. Peter Seitz, "The Mediator: Who He Is, What He Does, and How to Use Him," *People at Work: The Human Element in Modern Business*, AMA Management Report No. 1 (New York: American Management Associations, 1957), p. 91.
22. Arthur S. Meyer, "Function of the Mediator in Collective Bargaining," *Industrial & Labor Relations Review* 12, No. 3 (January, 1960), p. 161.
23. 37LA335.
24. Jules J. Justin, "Arbitrability and the Arbitrator's Jurisdiction," *Management Rights and the Arbitration Process*, Proceedings of the Ninth Annual Meeting, National Academy of Arbitrators. Copyright © 1959 by the Bureau of National Affairs, Inc., Washington, D.C. 20037. Reprinted by permission.
25. Walter E. Baer, *Grievance Handling: 101 Guides for Supervisors* (New York: American Management Associations, 1970).
26. *Local 174, Teamsters Union* v. *Lucas Flour Company*, 369 U.S. 95 (1962).
27. For full coverage of grievance procedures and their administration, see Walter E. Baer, *Grievance Handling: 101 Guides for Supervisors* (New York: American Management Associations, 1970).
28. "General Motors' First Proposal, 1973," Bureau of National Affairs Bulletin 735 (August 2, 1973).

29. Section 301 (a) Labor Management Relations Act, 29 U.S.C. 185 (a).
30. 363 U.S. 574, 40-LC-66,629 (1960).
31. 363 U.S. 564 (1960).
32. 363 U.S. 593 (1960).
33. "Two Collective Bargaining Negotiations and Contracts," Bureau of National Affairs Bulletin 77 (1971).
34. Owen Fairweather, "Employer Actions and Options in Response to Strikes in Breach of Contract," Proceedings of NYU Eighteenth Annual Conference on Labor (Washington: Bureau of National Affairs, 1966).
35. "Basic Patterns in Union Contracts," Bureau of National Affairs Bulletin 670 (February 4, 1971).
36. Ibid.
37. 369 U.S. 95, 44 LC Para. 50,470 (1962).
38. 57 Wash. 2d 95, 356 P. 2d 1(41-LC-50,076).
39. 359 U.S. 236 (37-LC-65,367).
40. 57 Wash. 2d at 102, 356 P. 2d at 5.
41. Stat. 156 (1947), 29 U.S.C. Sec. 185(a) (1958).
42. *Textile Workers* v. *Lincoln Mills*, 353 U.S. 448, 32-LC-70,733 (1957).
43. 363 U.S. 574, 40-LC-66,629 (1960).
44. Paul Jacobs, *Old before Its Time: Collective Bargaining at 28* (Center for the Study of Democratic Institutions, 1963).
45. Harold W. Davey, "Arbitration as a Substitute for Other Legal Remedies," *Labor Law Journal*, October, 1972. Reprinted by permission of *Labor Law Journal*, a Commerce Clearing House publication.
46. 27LA321; 28LA121; 24LA761.
47. 62-1 ARB 8164.
48. 62-3 ARB 8838. For other cases, see 62-2 ARB 8484; 61-1 ARB 8006; and 62-3 ARB 8923.
49. 29LA646.
50. 61-1 ARB 8020. For other cases, see 61-2 ARB 8308; 62-2 ARB 8355; 62-2 ARB 8583; 62-2 ARB 8678; and 62-3 ARB 9025.
51. 4LA744; 21LA421; 16LA99; 21LA843; 21LA239; 9LA447;

42LA142; 42LA328; 42LA923; 13LA304; 30LA181; 30LA250.

52. 28LA369; 35LA699; 20LA875; 33LA488; 6LA414.
53. 28LA782; 16LA99; 29LA622; 43LA608; 8LA758; 30LA109; 30LA562; 30LA250; 34LA325; 34LA607; 33LA594; 13LA143; 6LA617; 13LA295; 14LA475; 7LA648. For a contrary view, see 33LA807.
54. Arbitrator Ralph T. Seward carries this concept further. See 14LA988.
55. 17LA227; 7LA583; 24LA95; 29LA23.
56. 16LA317.
57. Harold W. Davey, "Arbitration as a Substitute for Other Legal Remedies," *Labor Law Journal,* October, 1972. Reprinted by permission of *Labor Law Journal,* a Commerce Clearing House publication.
58. 41LA214.
59. 41LA619.
60. 42LA95.
61. 33LA574.
62. 83LRRM1443.
63. 5LRRM806; 16LRRM501; 23LRRM1380; 35LRRM1265.
64. 80LRRM2165.
65. 82LRRM3025.
66. 74LRRM2257.
67. 79LRRM2555.
68. 80LRRM2680.
69. For example, see 172 F. Supp. 354, 360–362 (D.C.N.J. 1959), 43LRRM2868; 29LRRM2271; 32LRRM2270; 36LRRM2578; 58LRRM2568; 49LRRM2346; 40LRRM2113; 40LRRM2709; 41LRRM2709; 49LRRM2717; 59LRRM2427; 56LRRM1194.
70. 38LA1185.
71. 43LA450.
72. 22LA792.
73. 25LA474.
74. 25LA343.
75. 45LA366.
76. 4LRRM515.

77. 25LA270.
78. 45LA490.
79. 31LRRM2432. For the extension of this rule, see 33LRRM1114.
80. 42LA626; see also 45LA522.
81. 35LA757.
82. 41LA52.
83. 45LA826.
84. 37LRRM2673; 38LRRM2717.
85. For a full listing of the labor cases in which the court took final action during the term, see 83LRR227.
86. 83LRRM2189.
87. 81LRRM2853.
88. 83LRRM2183.
89. 65LRRM2449.
90. 81LRRM2001.
91. 83LRR2827, BNA, Inc.
92. 82LRRM1525.
93. 54LRRM1429.
94. "Why White-Collar Workers Can't Be Organized," *Harper's*, August, 1957.
95. 48LA203.
96. "Picketers Smash Restaurant after Nine Hurt at Job Site," Birmingham *Post Herald*, February 14, 1974.
97. I. W. Abel, "Basic Steel's Experimental Negotiating Agreement," based on a paper presented at the Fifth Annual Collective Bargaining Forum of the Institute of Collective Bargaining and Group Relations, *Monthly Labor Review*, September, 1973, p. 40. Reprinted by permission of the Institute of Collective Bargaining and Group Relations, Inc., and the *Monthly Labor Review*.
98. Charles T. Douds, "Labor Peace in Switzerland," *Labor Law Journal*, September, 1963, 806–808.

INDEX

A&P, Acme, and Food Fair Stores, no-strike clause, 90
Abel, I. W., 190
Abrahams, Harry, 115
Allied Industrial Workers Union, no-strike clause, 93–94
Allis Chalmers case, 142, 143
Amalgamated Street Railway Union, 200
American Arbitration Association, 29, 33
arbitrators, 30–32
expedited arbitration rules, 231–234
American Meat Institute, 175
Anderson Electric Co., mediation and arbitration clause, 50–51

arbitration
contract clause, 75–82
on crossing picket lines, 135–137
expedited procedure, 82–84, 203–207, 231–234
last-offer, 185–192
vs. mediation, 49–53
recent history, 27–28
voluntary, 25–27
arbitrator(s)
contract benefits denial ruling, 112–114
discharge and discipline ruling, 107–109
function, 28–29
growth in demand for, 34–35
identified, 29–32
injunctions and damages rulings, 114–116

251